Study, Power and
the University

SRHE and Open University Press Imprint
General Editor: Heather Eggins

Current titles include:

Study, Power and the University

Sarah J. Mann

Society for Research into Higher Education
& Open University Press

Open University Press
McGraw-Hill Education
McGraw-Hill House
Shoppenhangers Road
Maidenhead
Berkshire
England
SL6 2QL

email: enquiries@openup.co.uk
world wide web: www.openup.co.uk

and Two Penn Plaza, New York, NY 10121-2289, USA

First published 2008

A catalogue record of this book is available from the British Library

ISBN-13: 978-0-33-522113-4 (pb) 978-0-33-522114-1 (hb)
ISBN-10: 0-33-522113-0 (pb) 0-33-522114-9 (hb)

Library of Congress Cataloging-in-Publication Data
CIP data applied for

Typeset by RefineCatch Limited, Bungay, Suffolk
Printed in the UK by Bell and Bain Ltd, Glasgow

Fictitious names of companies, products, people, characters and/or data that may be used herein (in case studies or in examples) are not intended to represent any real individual, company, product or event.

The *McGraw·Hill* Companies

In loving memory of my parents, Sheila and Tony Mann

Contents

List of figures and tables

List of figures

List of tables

Acknowledgements

This book has taken me four years to write. I would not have managed to complete it, or even get going, without the help and support of a number of people.

First of all, I would like to thank all those anonymous students whose voices populate Chapter 3 of this book through quotations I have taken from published research or some of my own unpublished data.

I would also like to thank the researchers of these studies for permission to include these quotations in this book. They include Amy Bergerson, Sally Bradley, Penny Burke, Jenni Case, Sue Clegg, Miriam David, Nikki Dibben, Mary Fuller, Yannis Gabriel, Trevor Gale, Scherto Gill, Jackie Goode, Dot Griffiths, Tamsin Haggis, Tony Harland, Neil Harrison, Angela Johnson, Catherine Lambert, Susan Lea, Teresa Lillis, Delia Marshall, Erica McAteer, Stephanie McClure, Erja Moore, Marie Moreau, Barbara Read, Sheila Riddell, Delia Langa Rosado, Sabine Severiens, Karen Smith, Lyn Tett, Liz Thomas, Susan Weil, Naomi White, Paula Wilcox, and Rachel Zhou.

I would like to acknowledge permission to use a phrase from Kathleen Jamie's *Mr and Mrs Scotland are Dead: Poems 1980–1994* (Bloodaxe Books, 2002).

I owe a special thanks to my colleague and one-time boss Bob Matthew. I would not have got underway with this book, or had the space and time to complete it, without his unstinting encouragement, support and protection.

I would also like to thank *all* my colleagues at what used to be the Teaching and Learning Service at the University of Glasgow for their forbearance at my sometimes distraction, and for their encouragement and understanding along the way. Ros Ivanič at Lancaster University has also kindly offered friendship, support and encouragement which I have greatly appreciated as did Jean Barr and Alison Phipps at Glasgow University.

I would also like to thank Jennifer Rotherham and Shona Mullen at the Open University Press/McGraw-Hill for their encouragement, feedback and advice on questions I raised.

I have had feedback on different versions of the manuscript over the past four years. My thanks first of all to those anonymous reviewers, including as I now know, Moira Peelo at Lancaster University, who kindly took time to read my proposal and early chapters and offer me invaluable feedback and advice.

I also owe a special thanks to Glynis Cousin who has always encouraged me to write and took time, at a difficult time in her own life, to read the draft of the book and offer me constructive and very perceptive feedback which contributed to significant improvements in the book.

Finally, I would not have begun, nor managed to sustain this project without the unswerving love, encouragement and support of my husband Mike Breen. He also took on the role of critical – and friendly – reader and as ever gave me detailed, constructive and highly pertinent feedback which helped me significantly to enhance the existing manuscript.

Whilst there is no doubt that the support, encouragement and feedback of colleagues, friends and family have contributed to what is good in the book, any faults that remain are entirely my own responsibility.

1
Introduction

Universities have experienced significant pressures over the past few decades. The global predominance of a neo-liberal free market ideology and rapid developments in communications technology have created greater competition between institutions, in the context of decreased government funding, increasing student numbers, and performance-related research funding (Kreber, 2006; Maassen and Cloete, 2006: 7). Allied to this has been a greater requirement on universities to contribute to the social justice agenda through widening access and inclusive curricula, and to publicly account for, and enhance, the quality of their educational provision. Such pressures suggest a shift in status for many universities from autonomous institutions to service providers, accountable to the interests of multiple stakeholders – government, employers, students, staff, and regional bodies (Maassen and Cloete, 2006: 14).

Academic leaders are encouraged, and sometimes trained, to see their roles as managerial, and a new class of professional non-academic managers has been appointed in senior roles to promote efficiency and the achievement of government policy requirements (Lambert and Parker, 2006: 470; Maassen and Cloete, 2006: 16). There is a greater emphasis on performance, the measurability of outcomes, and the use of student satisfaction surveys to 'test' educational quality (Kreber, 2006: 7). In an effort to raise funds and secure their economic base, universities are becoming hybrid public/private institutions, diversified according to size, scope, student body, regional specialisation, and research/teaching emphasis (Houston and Lebeau, 2006: 8; Maassen and Cloete, 2006: 16). This economic uncertainty has also increased the vulnerability of universities to corporate interests through business investment in research and employer interest in the curriculum (Washburn, 2005; Kreber, 2006: 7).

Competing discourses, and purposes, between those of 'access', 'widening participation', 'inclusion', 'diversity', 'collegiality', 'inquiry', 'enhancement' and those of 'market', 'efficiency', 'performance', 'enterprise', 'employability' express the tensions between a social justice agenda and economic and managerial imperatives (Barnett, 2005: 791; Riddell et al., 2005: 636; Longden, 2006). Peseta (2007) argues that there has been a narrowing of the vision of the purpose of higher education curricula towards the achievement of learning outcomes and the production of employable graduates. Such narrowing is viewed by Cranmer (2006) as losing sight of the goal of developing the wider potential of the individual so that they may more generally contribute to society. Furthermore, increases in student numbers have led to large class sizes and a reduction in contact between academics and students particularly in the early years of the undergraduate degree programme which has limited the scope of human relations within the curriculum and the possibility of responding to individual needs within the more diverse student body.

Economic, policy, and stakeholder interests can thus be seen to exert a conflicting field of tension over the core teaching and research activities of universities. At worst, these conflicting demands undermine universities' capacities to undertake their core activities, at best the challenges they offer invite creative responses which enhance and transcend existing purposes and practices. The individual who has chosen to study at university level enters into this context in its various instantiations. And in an echo of the pressures on the institution, students experience their own particular pressures, and the tension between the exercise of their own autonomy and the need to conform to curricular and institutional requirements.

According to Robotham and Julian, 'the impact of stress [on students] is on a scale that cannot be ignored' (2006: 114). Key stressors include assessment, time and workload pressures, financial problems, new eating and sleeping arrangements, part-time work, new responsibilities, "meeting new people, career decisions, fear of failure, parental pressure" and general adjustment to leaving home, living in a foreign country and establishing a new life (2006: 110). Swaner (2007) also identifies substance misuse and depression as key problems in the US student population.

A shift in government policy from social to individual private funding of higher education, exemplified by the withdrawal of maintenance grants and the introduction of tuition fees in England and Wales, has had an impact on the time students have available to study. Part-time term-time employment has become commonplace. According to Callender and Wilkinson (2003) 64 to 70% of students are engaged in work during the academic year, and 63% of Scottish students from disadvantaged areas are engaged in part-time work, often involving long and unpredictable hours (Forsyth and Furlong, 2003).

Despite widening access policies and increasing student numbers, research suggests that social inequality continues to be a problem in higher education (Moreau and Leathwood, 2006a, b; Hebel, 2007; McDonough and Fann, 2007). In the United States for example, there is concern that ethnic minority groups are still under-represented in higher education and that students of colour are not completing degrees (Carter, 2006; McClure, 2006). In recent research on students with disabilities in the UK, the researchers conclude that whilst improvements have occurred, the 'greatest beneficiaries of this expansion [numbers of disabled students in higher education] have been disabled students from the most socially advantaged groups' (Riddell et al., 2005: 641).

Houston and Lebeau (2006: 4) also note the effects of fees and student loans on the lack of students from non-middle-class backgrounds taking up increased student places and the impact of this on social and geographical mobility.

While current policy may promise students greater say in their educational experience through the foregrounding of student consumer power, such policy also supports an instrumentalist position vis à vis the degree, framing the student as a future employee whose task is to develop responsibility and self-management along the academic way. According to Houston and Lebeau (2006), the diverse paths students take through higher education form a highly individualised experience, which in Moreau and Leathwood's conceptualisation lead to the 'neglect of social inequality' (2006b: 305), and the location of responsibility for student success and employment with the individual.

The current context of higher education is thus defined by a tension between the values of social justice, support for the realisation of individual potential through higher education, social and educational inclusion, and lifelong learning opportunities, and the harder, material necessities of a neo-liberal ideology supporting commercialisation, economic value criteria, competition, performance and consumption. Students, universities and academics are caught up within these conflicting and potentially alienating tensions. Given the pressures each are under, it is in many ways surprising how successful higher education can be in the student experience. For example one student describes her experience in the following way:

> I am quite a shy person and normally haven't the confidence to speak out, so I really can't fully express to you the excitement I feel when in the group I manage to 1) read out a . . . sentence 2) can't stop talking, as due to lack of group interaction that I have experienced until now, my nervous excitement is slightly unhinged . . . [the subject] really is changing my life – for the first time ever I feel normal and part of something (Ta for that!)
>
> (1st year mature female student, Arts, entry in weekly journal, week 8)[1]

and a report comparing the 2005 and 2006 National Student Surveys (NSS) in England, Wales and Northern Ireland concludes that students express 'high levels of satisfaction' with higher education courses (Surridge, 2007a: 10). At its best therefore higher education[2] engages the student in learning which is

> active, integrative of experience, marked by increasingly complex ways of knowing and doing, interactive with social contexts, and holistic in its encompassment of multiple domains of the self . . . [also] the

development of students' civic capacities for democratic participation and responsible engagement in community life . . .

(Swaner, 2007: 19)

It also aims to teach the capacity for critical thinking and questioning which Marshall and Case see as the defining feature of what makes higher education 'higher', '. . . crucial for maintaining an open and democratic society' (2005: 262).

However, such outcomes and positive experiences may not always be the case. Although the recent expansion of higher education has the potential to contribute to the emancipatory project of the *Long Revolution* proposed by Raymond Williams in 1961, 'a cultural revolution [which] extend[ed] the active process of learning, with the skills of literary and other advanced communication, to all people rather than to limited groups', it seems that higher education may be failing in this (Williams, in Couldry, 2000: 26).

The results of the NSS are based on a 56.5% response rate, in other words on just over half of the potential respondent population. And those least likely to respond include young mature students (22–30 years on entry), black or Asian students, and international students (Surridge, 2007b: 4). Of students responding, black and Asian students are less positive about their experience than white students, and whilst Teaching and Learning receives an overall mean score of 3.98, Assessment and Feedback scores less highly with 3.49 (on a five point scale) (2007b: 4). Whilst the NSS findings indicate variation in the student rating of satisfaction across institutions and subjects, the scale of the survey does not allow for variation in individual student satisfaction, nor for variation in experience across the timeframe of the degree. Some students feel unsupported and many students may feel this at some times. Such feelings may also be related to social inequality and the experience of difference (Davis et al., 2004; Wilcox et al., 2005; Hutchings, 2006; Porter and Swing, 2006). Where this goes wrong, it can lead to the student leaving the university:

no support, too much of a heavy workload, thinking that I was losing control in everything that I was studying

(Thomas and Quinn, 2007: 89)

And where students stay and succeed to attain a degree, some may have failed to achieve their full potential and an enlivened engagement with learning. This is evidenced in a number of ways.

Cousin (2003) argues that 'conventional academic testing' produces in students who find subject matter challenging – either in complexity or in relation to their values and attitudes – what she calls 'faking it' or 'mimicry', allowing the student to 'pass' without necessarily taking on the full implications of the subject for their understanding of the world and of others, their identity and emotions (in Meyer and Land, 2005).

Hofer, in a review of studies of the development of students' personal epistemologies, writes that 'college . . . has some small but measurable impact on epistemological development', and concludes that most students leave university lacking the capacity to solve ill-structured problems, and go beyond absolutist or multiplist thinking (2001: 369).

This wasting of potential can be established in the first year of study where there may be minimal interaction with academics in informal small group contexts allied with student inability to understand how to use any free time for study (Longden, 2006). According to Longden this 'presents a picture of academic boredom' in the early years (2006: 179) and 'students without a strong academic background and little evidence of a well-developed learning autonomy are likely to set lower academic horizons than would otherwise be wished by the academic community' (2006: 181).

Studies which investigate student approaches to learning consistently find a significant number of students within the research sample reporting the adoption of surface approaches, in other words approaches to learning which seek to meet task requirements through memorisation and reproduction strategies and which are associated with the desire to get tasks done and out of the way. For example, Heikkilä and Lonka report that 190 students out of a total sample of 366 from across disciplines and levels adopt surface approaches combined with 'task-irrelevant behaviour' and indicate problems with the 'regulation of learning' (2006: 110). In a study of 1279 first year students in the Netherlands, Vermunt reports a range of 'learning patterns' adopted by students, including reproduction-directed learning and undirected learning, and concludes that students tend to restrict how they approach the processing of new knowledge where their examinations do not require 'critical learning' (2005: 231). A recent study by Norton et al. shows how this effect of context on approach is also experienced by academics. In a study of teachers' beliefs and intentions in higher education, the researchers conclude that teachers' intentions 'reflect a compromise between teachers' conceptions of teaching and their academic and social contexts' (2005: 537).

Higher education thus has the potential to enable a rich and engaged learning experience which leads to personal transformation, an enlarged understanding of the world and a capacity to act in it in positive and reflexive ways. It can also alienate, waste opportunity and limit potential. It can undermine or diminish the individual, is implicated in issues of social inequality, and can reinforce or create in the student an approach to learning which seeks to satisfy and survive curricular requirements. It can also constrain academic teachers in the pedagogic intentions and practices they adopt. It thus creates pedagogic spaces which restrict autonomy and the generation and deployment of creative energy and in which the student can avoid personal commitment to their programme of study.

A basic assumption of this book therefore is that higher education is neither neutral nor natural. It affects people's lives, it is implicated in relations of power within society, and the way it is organised and undertaken is a function of social and historical choices. Study is thus a social practice which has empowering or alienating psychological and social consequences for the individual. The book thus explores the inter-relationship between study, power and the university through the dynamic interaction between the individual student and the institution as this is mediated through the play of power in the different contextual layers the university is enmeshed in – its social and economic function in society, its structuring of time, space and activity, its discoursal practices, and its validating and assessing functions.

Why have I written this book?

I do not come to this project from a disinterested position. My concern with issues of power, alienation and agency in education arises from my own particular educational biography.

I am a white, middle-class, middle-aged woman. I had a privileged early education. I attended the Alliance Française in Santiago between the ages of five and eight, and continued my French education at the Lycée Français de Londres until I was 13 years old. Disaster struck when my parents deemed it necessary to introduce me to the English educational system by sending me to boarding school.

I found myself completely at sea in this new environment with only French educational values to sustain me. I was used to an individualist, secular and intellectual ethos, in which sports, teams, uniforms and prayers had no place. I wrote the following poem about my schooling in April of my last year at this English boarding school. It was 1972, I was 18 years old and was about to do my A levels.[3]

Dirt Track
You dragged me through the dirt to the end of the road
Over jagged stones and dry, relentless sand.
You fed me on gravel, washed down with salt water,
And at every turning of the path was a way
To greener land, to soft sweet water,
To euphoria and forgetfulness, to freedom and myself.
But at every turning you had set up grey
Barricades, justified by forbidding signs
'No Time' 'No Entry' 'Not For You'.
And you pushed me up the path
And you whispered in my ear,
'It's all for your own good.
      It will stand you in good stead.'
At the last bend I spat back what you
Had given me; it had rotted in my head.
And there you left me, with a sack of rubble
On my back.
And with nowhere to dump my sack of
Rubble there ahead.

Although I was successful at school, I hated it. It left me with a feeling of having been shut up – literally, as it was a boarding school, and metaphorically, as I felt I had attained success through simply reproducing what was required. I usually knew 'the answers', as long as it was not mathematics or science.

That autumn I went to university, unclear as to why I was going except to pursue a course of study that was of interest to me and to have a good time – to be 'out of school'. Early on, as part of being welcomed, I met the Dean for a chat. He told me that just because I had two As and a B at A level, it did not mean that I would be a successful student. I was crushed. Hadn't I done well? Wasn't this what they wanted? Maybe I wasn't so good after all.

Although I cannot attribute the rest of my experience at university to this one remark, it is certainly the case that I lost significant academic confidence at this point. I seemed to be moving in a mysterious space which was quite 'other' to me. It was possible to get by, by using the strategies I had adopted previously at school, but I certainly did not feel engaged in a process I was in charge of and could participate in with others. I was feeling shut up again and for the first time shut out, but for different reasons. This time I was afraid to speak up, shy of being 'stupid', and did not know how to join the conversation. I did manage to do some good work, and even got an A once. This was usually when the task allowed me to be the author of my own expertise and to create something new, rather than required me to demonstrate my understanding. I left university with a 2:2.

Meanwhile I had trained as an English as a Foreign Language Teacher to fulfil the requirement of my degree to do a year abroad. I learnt through my short intensive training and through my subsequent practice that the teacher could act and create a context in which it was possible to be enlivened and engaged and in which it was possible for students to talk with each other and cooperate together. Why hadn't this been possible at school or at university?

I returned to university a few years later in order to pursue a Masters degree in Linguistics. I was lucky to have been accepted that year by an admissions tutor who wanted 'gender balance' in the group. This time I thrived. I learnt what it was to have a brain; to be intellectually engaged; to read and think critically; and even to be able to write. This experience was profoundly liberating for me.

Blake et al. (2003: 5) describe the educational philosophy of Hirst and Peters (1970) as one which argues: 'It is necessarily the case that education for citizens of a liberal democracy is unproblematic and non-ideologic. It aims to equip such citizens with what they need to participate in such a democracy.'

More than anything else my educational biography has given me a contrary view. It has left me with a profound feeling that learning in institutional settings can be either stultifying and diminishing, or enlivening, and sometimes life-changing. I do not think I am alone in this experience.

It has also left me with a keen sense that power – for example, who/what has the power to decide what is done and how, who has the power to decide who is 'good' or 'bad', who a 'success', who a 'failure' – and how this plays itself out in the conjunction between the individual and the institution, is a key issue.

Why is power significant?

This concern with power and education is nothing new. In education generally a number of educational theorists have examined the way power maintains and reproduces existing social relations in society and supports the continuation of the capitalist system through the nature of the curriculum, academic knowledge and discourse, and social and pedagogic relations.[4]

Within the field of higher education, Becker et al. (1968) published an ethnographic study of the student experience at the University of Kansas in which they concluded that power permeated student life. Whilst students exerted some power within the 'political and organizational' life of the university through student governing bodies, and were relatively autonomous within the sphere of their own private lives, in academic matters they were 'subject' to college faculties and administrators. In the introduction to a re-issue of this book, Becker argues that students responded to this subject position by adopting what Scott (1985) has termed the 'weapons of the weak', in other words the establishment of a culture in opposition to the dominating culture which enables those subject to it to survive (Becker, 1995). In this case, students adopted a 'Grade Point Average' culture of finding ways to obtain the highest possible grades. Becker (1995) refers to a subsequent study of student cultures by Horowitz (1987: 118) which positions students as subject to 'a society [the university] in which they did not make or enforce the rules. . . . In this way they had much in common with workers, slaves and prisoners'.

In the 1970s, a number of studies were published in the UK which, whilst not directly addressing the issue of power in the student experience, nevertheless sought to understand this experience as something that arises out of complex social and institutional contexts, for example Miller and Parlett (1974) on the student experience of examinations; Parlett (1977) on the learning milieu of academic departments; and Laurillard (1978) on the context of learning. Elton and Laurillard (1979) offer a review of these studies.

The French sociologist Pierre Bourdieu and his colleagues have explored the relationship between higher education, agency, social relations and power in Bourdieu (1988), Bourdieu and Passeron (1977), and Bourdieu et al. (1994). More recently, a focus on academic literacies (for example, Lea and Street, 1998) raises the issue of power in relation to the academic tasks students have to undertake. Lillis (2001) writing within this tradition argues for academic writing to be seen as an institutionally produced and privileged essayist literacy practice. Similarly, researchers such as Anderson and Williams (2001) and Read et al. (2003) investigate the workings of power in the normative and excluding nature of higher education for non-traditional students. And in the United States, Margolis et al. (2001) offer a collection of papers that each argue for the powerful conservative effects of higher education on maintaining existing social hierarchies and undermining social resistance and change.

However, much of current dominant literature on the student experience in higher education focuses on what I would call the *psycho-pedagogical* context of student learning. Such work tries to understand why students approach learning in the ways that they do by investigating the interaction between the psychological world of the learner and the pedagogic context (see for example, Marton et al., 1997; Prosser and Trigwell, 1999; Biggs, 2003). This approach owes a considerable debt to 'phenomenography', an approach to investigating the experience of learning adopted by Marton (1981) in order to counter predominant cognitivist or behaviourist approaches (see also Booth, 1997; Entwistle, 1997). The phenomenographic approach seeks to build on the phenomenological assumption that the world can only be known through a relational epistemology, which assumes that knower and object are inextricably bound. Neither subject, nor object have priority. The knowing subject is always a knowing subject of something. This position attempts to move away from the dualism set up between subject and object by the Cartesian view of the reasoning subject which gives priority to mind (cognitivist theories of learning), and by the empiricist Humean position which gives priority to the object (behaviourist theories of learning) (Morrow and Torres, 2002: 22). As the focus is on the subject as an experiencing subject of the world, phenomenography also significantly gives priority to data from students' accounts of their experience, rather than from the testing of hypotheses of assumed learning behaviours or processes (Marton, 1981). Whilst the early research on student learning which became the basis for phenomenography focused on students' approaches and outcomes in learning from text, phenomenographic studies now tend to focus on students' conceptions of the subject matter to be learned and of different learning contexts such as tutorials and, where appropriate, the relationship between these and student approach (Booth, 1997; Entwistle, 1997; Ashwin, 2005).

Phenomenographic research has made a significant contribution to our understanding of student learning by highlighting the *situated* nature of learning in higher education from what students say about their experience. This is best summarised by Prosser and Trigwell's constitutionalist model of student learning. According to Prosser and Trigwell (1999: 13–14), this model describes how at any one time the individual student's particular approach to learning emerges out of the inter-relationship between the student's past experience (what they bring to the learning context), the particular context of learning (including the teacher's contribution) and the student's perception of their situation. A distinction is thus drawn between the actual context and the student's unique situation, as constituted by their perceptions of the context. In this way, phenomenography's theorisation of the individual-in-context is primarily psychological (student perceptions) and pedagogical (teaching and learning context).

What is not directly addressed in this approach are the issues I raise in my educational biography, namely the socially situated nature of the individual, born into and living within particular material conditions, social relations, and cultural and discoursal contexts; the institutional context of studying and learning;[5] and the ways in which power permeates the teaching and learning practices of individual students, teachers and the institution. I argue that what is important is the need to hold onto the significance and complexity of the individual student's experience and at the same time use socially informed theory in order to understand how it might arise. Morrow and Torres (2002: 18) in their analysis of the similarities and differences between Habermas' and Freire's views of the individual, society and education, suggest that Habermas wishes to move 'from the monological philosophy of consciousness [for example phenomenography] to an intersubjective communicative paradigm', in which a critical social science will offer both a hermeneutic and an analytic social knowledge (Morrow and Torres, 2002: 58); in other words, a knowledge which integrates interpretation of subjective experience with analysis of social structures. In short, a critical social science presupposes a kind of '*quasi-causal* structural analysis of *depth interpretation* [of consciousness of agents] that illuminates the constraining and enabling effects of material (institutional) realities.' (Thompson, 1981, in Morrow and Torres, 2002: 58–9, original emphasis).

More recently Couldry (2000: 114 and 128) has argued for a repositioning and refocusing of Cultural Studies – the concerns of which are the relationship between the individual, culture and power – in such a way that it takes account of both personal experience and social theory. He draws on Probyn (1993: 3) to describe this as a process of 'thinking the cultural through the self'.

In essence, what I want to do in this book is to examine the relationship between study, power and the university in such a way that 'thinks the educational' and the institutional forces of enablement and alienation, 'through the self'. By this I mean thinking theory *through* individual student accounts and my own experience. In this, I align myself with the following statement by Blake and Masschelein (2003: 39) concerning critical theory:

> Critical Theory is distinctive in claiming that the theorists' involvement and engagement in the reality under investigation is not an obstacle to, but a prerequisite of, their 'objectivity'. Objectivity is not achieved by theoretical distance from phenomena, but by personal closeness to them.

Some basic assumptions

In writing this book, I have made certain basic assumptions. These are presented in this section in order to help us get under way. The rest of the book will be an elaboration and development of these ideas.

The individual's potential to learn

Each individual has the potential to learn. They have the potential to be able to do things they cannot yet do and to investigate and make sense of the world in which they live, and their position in it, in ways which they do not yet know. They have the potential to make explicit and critique what they normally take for granted and to contribute ways of acting, seeing and knowing the world which are not yet known. And they are able to act cooperatively and in dialogue with others.

Higher education's potential

Each individual has the right to an education that will support the realisation of these potentials. Such a realisation is a positive, enlivening good for the individual:

> . . . higher education is potentially a space in which to manage and transcend feelings of marginalization, meaninglessness and inauthenticity in interaction with others; in which it is possible, given their support and encouragement, to compose a new life, a different story and a more cohesive self.
>
> (West, 1996: 10)

Higher education is also a good for society. An active, participatory democracy depends on citizens who are inquisitive, critical, informed and engaged. Higher education has a key role to play in this:

> If man is essentially a learning, creating, communicating being, the only social organization adequate to his nature is a participating democracy in which all of us, as unique individuals, learn, communicate and control.
>
> (Williams, 1961, in Couldry, 2000: 26)

Learning and studying

Whilst the educational purpose of higher education is to enable learning in its students – both in terms of process and outcome, the practices which students undertake in order to achieve this learning can best be described as study or studying. The term 'learning' captures the implicit and to a certain extent natural psychological processes which lead to change in conception and understanding, whereas 'study' refers to the practices – such as reading, note-taking, essay writing and so on, which universities require students to do for the purposes of achieving and assessing this learning. The tension explored in this book is between learning and studying – how the institutionalisation of learning as studying brings power into play in the student experience of, and engagement with, learning.

The individual is a member of a differentiated society

The socio-structural position the individual occupies (class, gender, ethnicity, age, culture) will be significant for the individual to the extent that their social, cultural and financial resources match – or fail to match – those taken for granted by the institution. Those for whom there is a relatively seamless match are likely to be privileged over those for whom this is not so. Those for whom the match is not seamless are more likely to struggle within the higher education context (though not necessarily so), and others may never have the chance to get near it.[6] Whilst recognising this potential effect of privilege, I am also assuming that how this is experienced and responded to will vary according to each individual and cannot be reduced to the effects of a particular class or gender (Webb, 2001: 53).

Agency

Each individual brings their own unique biography and experience to a particular educational context. This biography and experience will be shaped by the material and socio-cultural conditions and relations through which they have lived, *and* by the individual's particular perception and interpretation of these. This interaction between individual and context is not static but historical and dynamic. It takes place over time and involves an unfolding of the past and the future in the experience of the present. Agency arises in the capacity of the individual to make sense of their own particular circumstances in their own way *and* in the individual's capacity to transform these. Such action can be both individual and collective. Thus, rather than viewing individuals as either determined by wider social forces or fully in control of determining themselves, individuals can be seen to be co-constitutive of society and of themselves within society, what Gough and Madill (2007) refer to as 'complex subjectivity'. This perspective allows for the possibility of individual and social change. Such potentiality was seen by Camus to be what makes us human:

> They stood up because it was the human thing to do. They stood up because there was some violation of their souls that was so deep they had to rebel. It was existential. . . . You rebel because you are human, to prove that you exist.
>
> (Tom Hayden in Terkel, 2003: 62, concerning Jewish people in the Warsaw Ghetto and with reference to Camus)

Contained here are two ways of thinking of the self – as an inviolable and essential being whose 'soul' rebels, or as a complex, differentiated, and fragmented being produced by a unique biography and the specific and changing contexts of situation through which they live. Spivak suggests that we are in some senses both of these, and that the requirement to be heard, to challenge and to transform is founded on an assertion of respect for one's own humanity and that of others:

> I cannot in fact clean my hand and say 'I'm specific'. In fact I must say that I'm an essentialist from time to time. . . . Strategically, one can look at essentialisms, not as descriptions of the way things are, but as something one must adopt to produce a critique of anything.
> (Spivak, 1990, in Sarup, 1996: 166)

In order to offer a critique of the role of the university in the student experience, I am assuming something essential about the nature of being human – the capacity for suffering that can arise where one's humanity and potential are limited. I am also assuming a diversity and uniqueness in the human experience and what individuals take to be meaningful, so that what may be experienced by one as limiting, may be experienced by another as liberating, and that this may change over time. I am also assuming that as individuals and as groups, human beings have the capacity to interpret, analyse, critique and transform their circumstances.

Alienation and engagement

As I have said earlier, education can have an engaging and positive effect on an individual's life. It can also have a negative and alienating effect. These experiences can be described as 'liberating' or 'emancipatory' and as 'oppressive', as either an opening up for the individual or a closing down – of opportunities, of potentialities, of ways of thinking and knowing, of confidence, and so on. And such a closing down of the self can lead to 'the estrangement . . . of the learner from what in higher education we might assume they should be involved in, namely, the subject and process of study itself' (Mann, 2001: 8), in other words can lead to alienation.[7] Despite postmodern criticism of the relevance of the concept of 'alienation' to understanding a world in which the very idea of the self is challenged,[8] for this reason I assert the relevance of the term for it captures the idea of potential, power and loss all in the one word.

Power and the institution

In day to day practice in higher education and in much educational research, the neutrality of the educational institution is taken for granted. Institutional processes, practices and norms are assumed to be normal and natural. Contrary to this, it is my contention that the processes and experiences of studying within institutions of education – the experience of alienation and engagement – cannot be understood without making visible the hidden workings of the institution and the ways in which power operates within these. This is important because these invisible processes can negatively influence learning by inhibiting individual potential, individual self-concept and confidence, or by disturbing the natural learning process through the coping strategies and study approaches that individuals adopt in order to attain institutionally defined success.

In summary, I am assuming that higher education has the capacity and potential to enable individuals to fulfil their potential as learners, but that this project can be undermined by the very institutional conditions within which this learning is undertaken. This book is an exploration of the ways in which the context of the institution – and the workings of power within it – can limit this potential. Rather like images seen through a kaleidoscope, the different accounts that can be given of higher education and student learning are multi-faceted and multi-coloured, made of many different aspects and factors. The image revealed by the turn of the kaleidoscope in this book highlights a critical stance towards the university as an institution of higher education.

Although I do not directly address the experience of academics in the institution, this does not mean that I am not mindful of the fact that their experience is also subject to its own pressures. My focus in this case however is on the student.

A note about the literature I draw on

I have used two kinds of literature in this book – literature that tells us something about the current context of higher education and the current student experience, and literature which presents different philosophical and theoretical concepts or frameworks. I have tried where possible with the former to include examples from 2005 upwards, and certainly from within the first decade of this century. With the latter, I have not restricted myself to a criterion of recency. Instead I have drawn on work that has been seminal in its contribution to the development of thinking in the field of higher education research and work which contributes significant philosophical or theoretical positions and conceptualisations relevant to my purpose.

The structure of the book

This book is in three parts. The first part gives an account of how students approach their learning in higher education and how they experience being a student. It suggests that this experience is best understood as situated within the institutional context of the university. Chapter 2 offers a review of the student-learning literature and the insights it can give us into the student's experience, whilst Chapter 3 gives voice to a more holistic account of this experience by drawing on student accounts from a range of qualitative studies. It brings to the fore the subjective experience of students – the hermeneutic aspect of the concerns of a critical social science, and emphasises the 'richness' of accounts of the student experience (Greasley and Ashworth, 2007).

The second part of the book examines the characteristics of the university as an institutional context for learning and the ways in which power is implicated within the student's experience of, and approach to, higher education. This highlights the analytical and social structural aspects of a critical social science. Chapter 4 offers a framework for conceptualising the institution as a context for learning and locates different theorisations of power within this. This framework highlights three levels of context: a macro societal level, the institutional level itself, and the micro context of any particular learning activity and encounter. From the macro perspective, Chapter 5 examines the economic and social functions of higher education and the effects of this on the student experience. This includes an examination of higher education's role in the reproduction of existing social relations in society and how this impacts on the student experience of identity and difference.

At the institutional level, Chapter 6 discusses the nature of institutions in themselves and develops this through an analysis of the hidden curriculum of higher education – the ways in which the institution as a context for learning inevitably produces an implicit curriculum that shapes the student experience in fundamental ways, including the particular effects that the institutionalisation of time, space and activity have for the self, and in particular learning and the student experience.

Moving to the micro level, Chapter 7 addresses the issue of language and the predominantly socio-discoursal and thus normative nature of studying and learning activity in the academy – listening to lectures, speaking in seminars, reading articles and books, writing essays and reports. The chapter analyses the ways in which the micro context of the immediate situation in which these practices take place and the wider macro cultural context of the institution and society impact on the student's capacity to develop a fluent voice within these communicative contexts. Finally, Chapter 8 focuses on the particular perspective that undertaking such activities within the context of assessment brings to the student experience and the student's capacity to actively and productively engage in them.

In the third part of the book, I summarise the implications of the institution as a context for learning for our understanding of the student experience and the challenges these pose for students, teachers and institutions. Chapter 9 outlines the limiting forces of concentration at work in the institution and how these impact on the student experience. The concluding chapter, Chapter 10, summarises the differentiating forces that seem to enable an enlivened, active and productive engagement in the learning process and proposes five conditions for supporting these.[9]

Who am I addressing?

I have four specific readers in mind – colleagues in the field of educational/ academic development in higher education and in the area of student support; fellow researchers and writers in the field of higher education who may also be educational developers, and/or academics in other disciplines; academic colleagues who are engaged in professional development courses in higher education, or who wish to further their understanding of the student experience; and more senior academic and management colleagues who have the power to potentially change the way things are done and organised within their institutions of higher education.

Whoever you are, I hope you will gain something from reading this book. My own hopes are that you might derive some of the following:

- a sense of what students are telling us about their experience in higher education
- a perspective on what we are doing in our institutions of higher education which might alienate or engage our students
- a theoretical analysis of how the relationship between the individual, the institution and wider society might produce these experiences
- an appreciation of the significance of power in helping us to inform our understanding and practice of higher education
- a perspective on how we could organise ourselves and do things better.

I believe that as higher education practitioners – teachers, researchers, administrators, policy makers, managers – we are implicated in the negative and positive consequences for students of higher education through the choices we make about how to organise learning and how to engage with our students. These choices express our stance towards our students as human beings and our stance towards the kind of society we live in and wish to produce. But we are also constrained in what we can do by the fact that our practice is set within an institutional and wider political, economic, cultural and social context. I hope that this book will go some way to helping us understand why things are the way they are, what we can and must change, and why this can also be so difficult.

Cautionary comments

The aim of this book is to provide a critical account of the role of the university as an institution in the student experience of higher education. In doing this, I run the risk of offering an overly deterministic account of the institution's effects on the individual and of positioning the student as victim. This is not my intention. I am well aware that many students find higher education satisfying and achieve success within it. However, a minority do not; and of those who are successful, and satisfied, the experience will contain highs and lows; and many in order to succeed will adopt coping strategies that undermine their own natural learning process and potential as learners. It is this effect on the student experience that arises in the inter-relationship between the individual and the institution which is of interest to me.

I am not aiming to present a new theory of learning or of the student experience. What I am aiming to do is to theorise the student experience in such a way that takes account of the issue of power and the ways in which the institution can both diminish and enhance students' lives.[10] To ignore the issues of power and control in any account of the student experience may be to ignore the most crucial aspects of the educational experience. To do so would be to ignore the kind of theory I need in order to account for my own experience as a student. And that I cannot do.

As Couldry says, in describing an accountability principle for cultural research:

> Quite simply: the language and theoretical framework with which we analyse others should always be consistent with, or accountable to, the language and theoretical framework with which we analyse ourselves.
>
> (Couldry, 2000: 126).

Part 1

The student experience

In the introduction I asserted the need to offer an account of the student experience in higher education which takes seriously the issue of power. I argued this on the assumption that higher education has the capacity to both empower and to oppress, and that mainstream and dominant texts on student learning in higher education tend to neglect this dimension of the student experience and the context of learning.

My purpose in this first part of the book is to make this case in more detail. In Chapter 2 I offer a review of a seminal text on student learning – *The Experience of Learning* – first published in 1984, but still highly influential today both in its methodological approach and in the findings summarised. This review has three purposes. First, I aim to demonstrate how necessary it is to understand the student learning experience as situated in context. Second, to show how the issue of power and the significance of the institution as a context for learning is implicitly present in these studies, even though not directly addressed. And third, to show that neglecting an explicit focus on the issue of power in the student learning experience silences the student voice as 'subjected' and in this way avoids the need to problematise the institution as a context for learning (Becker, 1995).

In Chapter 3, I address this last point by presenting a range of student voices that reveals what students say about the enlivening aspect of their experience as well as its opposite – its oppressive and subjected experience. In this way, I signal the significance of power in formal educational processes – how individuals who have come to an institution in order to be helped to learn can find themselves at different times empowered, energised and actively engaged, or powerless, apathetic, subject to the requirements of others and passively compliant. I try to identify particularly where, or in relation to what, this experience of powerlessness seems to be most felt.

This chapter then leads to the second part of the book in which I pursue the investigation of the institution of higher education as a context for study and learning.

2

Student approaches to learning

In this chapter I review the seminal contribution made by early research on student learning through a discussion of the findings presented in *The Experience of Learning* (Marton et al., 1997).[11] The significance of this text is that it brings together the work of a number of researchers who were investigating learning in higher education from the point of view of the student. The authors argue that this is the only way to make sense of the teaching and learning process in higher education (Entwistle, 1997). All other perspectives (that of teachers or of researchers) are from the outside in. What is necessary is a view from the inside out. The data that informs the researchers' perspective was therefore collected through in-depth interviews with students in either naturalistic (close to the natural situation of learning) or in natural settings, in other words actual educational settings. In analysing the data, the researchers also make the key assumption that the categories derived concerning, for example, 'approaches to learning' are not descriptive of invariant characteristics of the student but arise in the interaction between the student and the particular task they are engaged in. They are thus 'relational' concepts, which allow us to perceive a dynamic interplay between individual students and pedagogic contexts. The image of the student experience which emerges from this work is a complex one.

I explore this by first reviewing studies presented in *The Experience of Learning* which contribute to our understanding of the individual student's psychological context of learning and then studies which contribute to our understanding of aspects of the pedagogic context which are perceived as significant by students.

The psychological context of learning

Students vary in the reasons they have for studying at university. Some will have vocational reasons for study, others academic, personal or social reasons. Beaty et al. (1997) term these 'learning orientations' and distinguish between the four reasons according to whether they are experienced intrinsically or extrinsically. For example, a student with an academic orientation may be interested in study for itself (intrinsic) or to progress in their academic career (extrinsic). They also make the point that students may hold a number of orientations and that these may change over time (see also Morgan and Beaty in the same volume). The authors argue that these 'learning orientations' form the context within which students strategically negotiate an internal 'study contract' which influences the decisions they make about how to engage with the requirements of their degree programme and where to put their efforts.

At a more micro level, findings from studies in naturalistic settings investigating how students learn from texts indicate a relationship between how students conceive of the learning task, the approach they adopt, and the quality of their learning outcome. Those students who conceive of the task as seeking understanding are likely to adopt a deep approach to the task, and the outcome of their reading will be an understanding of the main points of the text, whereas students who conceive of the task as requiring the reproduction of knowledge adopt a surface approach focusing on memorisation of discrete information or facts in the text, and the outcome will indicate such reproduction (Marton and Saljo, 1997).[12] Whilst the analytic categories of 'surface' and 'deep' distinguish *what* the student focuses on – whether a student is seeking meaning or not, Svensson's (1997) 'atomistic' and 'holistic' categories distinguish *how* students organise their reading of the content of texts (Marton and Saljo, 1997: 47–8). These two aspects combine to form the meaning of what are now termed 'surface' and 'deep' approaches to learning.

Seeking to enrich their understanding of what influences students to adopt surface or deep approaches, Marton and Saljo explain unsuccessful attempts to induce a deep approach by drawing on Fransson (1977) to suggest that an interested and relaxed student is more likely to adopt a deep approach, whereas an anxious student who feels threatened and sees the task and/or text as irrelevant, is likely to adopt a surface approach. Marton and Saljo (1997: 55–7) also investigated the relationship between the conception a student has of learning in general and the particular approach they adopt. They argue that conceptions 1 and 2 in Saljo's 1979 scheme (see Figure 2.1) are associated with a surface approach, and conceptions 4 and 5 with a deep approach. Conception 3 is seen to be between the two.

Later work in natural settings (Beaty et al., 1997; Ramsden, 1997) identified a further 'strategic' approach in which the focus is on achieving marks through managing time and effort according to students' interpretations of course requirements, and their internal 'study contract'.

The picture that emerges from these studies is one in which students' general orientations, their conceptions of learning, their interest in and their definitions of the task to be undertaken, and their level of anxiety influence the approach they adopt and therefore their learning outcome. These could be said to form the psychological context of learning.

1. A quantitative increase in knowledge

2. Memorising

3. The acquisition, for subsequent utilisation, of facts, methods, and so on

4. The abstraction of meaning

5. An interpretative process aimed at understanding reality

Figure 2.1   Conceptions of learning (Saljo, 1979)

Although the studies reviewed here do not directly address the issue of power, it is nevertheless possible to see that bringing a perspective that includes power into this account of the student experience might help us to understand the student experience further. For example, whilst we might say that students will approach their study and learning in relation to a particular text because of their perceptions, personal study contract, and emotional state, the student does not act and exist in isolation from others and from the society in which they live. A conception of a learning task as requiring mere reproduction is likely to have arisen through previous experience of schooling, in which certain ways of revealing 'learning outcomes' are required by the teacher and the educational system. Feeling anxious suggests a concern for one's own existential state and for one's self-confidence and sense of self in the eyes of others. This is an effect of power – the effect on one's sense of self of how one assumes others may judge one. And finally, a strategic approach, whilst seeming to indicate an active approach to studying, nevertheless seems to be encouraged by the necessity to succeed within the particular requirements of the curriculum and of societal expectation.

The next section further examines the dynamic between the individual's psychological context and their approach to study by emphasising and elaborating on the role of students' perceptions of the pedagogic context itself.

The pedagogic context of learning

In a study which compares the relationship between students' meaning or reproducing orientations (general tendencies to adopt either deep or surface approaches respectively) with their perceptions of the quality of the learning environment, Ramsden suggests that students tend to adopt a reproducing orientation in academic departments which they perceive to 'combine heavy workload with a lack of choice over content and method' (1997: 214), and a meaning orientation in departments which 'were perceived to provide good teaching (and particularly help with studying) combined with freedom in learning (choice of study method and content)' (1997: 213).[13]

Negative perceptions of assessment are also identified by Ramsden as linked to reproducing orientations. Anxiety around assessment, perceptions of examinations and of marking schemes as requiring particular outcomes, the predictability of assessment requirements, and the experience of work-loads as overwhelming, combine to create a context in which students are more likely to adopt surface approaches (Ramsden, 1997: 203). Ramsden also reveals how attitudes to study are influenced by these perceptions, and how attitude and motivation combine to support or disrupt the student's engagement in their studies. A clear link is thus indicated here between pedagogic context, as interpreted by the student, and student approach and experience. Furthermore, it is clear from this research that the pedagogic context can be said to be exerting power over students by limiting the student's freedom through workload demands, restrictive and predictable assessment tasks, and prescribed teaching and learning methods – all of which seem to undermine a more active and inquiring approach to study.

Svensson's work helps us understand in more detail the interaction between student approach and curriculum and assessment demands. He draws a distinction between 'skill in learning' and 'skill in studying'. 'Skill in learning' is holistic, exhaustive and focused on meaning, involving 'open exploration and use of the possibilities inherent in the material, allied to a consideration of relevant previous knowledge' (1997: 68). He contrasts this with an atomistic approach which breaks things down into parts without organising these into an integrating whole, and argues that the biggest step in attaining skill in learning is to move from an atomistic to a holistic approach. However, the context of learning in higher education is such that more and more material is required to be learned – and examined – in shorter timeframes. The integrative character of the holistic approach allows the student to deal with larger amounts of material by focusing on key prin-ciples and themes, but the approach needs time. Thus failure 'may result from a devotion to thorough understanding' (1997: 71). On the other hand, a student who adopts an atomistic approach will be selective, achieving only a narrow understanding of particular aspects of the material to be learnt. Although this may end up being an effective 'skill in studying', for it may allow the student to satisfy assessment requirements, it will be disastrous for genuine learning. The implication here is that the pedagogic context, rather than supporting learning, is in fact most likely to subvert it.

This theme is amplified in Saljo's study, investigating further how students interpret texts. He concludes that it is '*the intention to learn from the text which leads people to misunderstand it*' (1997: 103, original emphasis). He argues that the conception someone has of learning will influence how they read a text for learning. Thus a student who conceives of learning as 'accumulating knowledge (by memorisation)' will adopt a surface approach to their read-ing which will disrupt what Saljo terms 'the communicative premise' by which people normally engage with texts – finding out what the author wants to make known. Setting the reading of a text in a learning context will for many people shift their normal meaning seeking approach to one that is focused on reproduction. Significantly, Saljo goes on to argue that this conception of learning has become normalised, for it is the one most commonly used in society and reproduced through schooling. This perspective allows us to see how the taken-for-granted assumptions that operate in society about learning find their way into the actual micro-process of reading a text in a pedagogic context. It is as if, in Saljo's terms, the normal figure-ground relationship between text and meaning in which meaning is the figure, is reversed when the activity of reading a text is placed in a pedagogic context. Part of what makes this pedagogic context significant is its contextualisation within the wider society. This suggests the operation of a more subtle effect of power.

Most people experience learning through schooling. This context is usually associated with the requirement to 'prove' one's learning capacity through exercises, tests and exams in which one has to reproduce one's memory of something taught or studied. Thus it is likely that the common-sense view of learning that circulates within society will be the one most associated with schooling and with memorisation and reproduction. Such a view of learning is also often taken for granted within the media. Popular television quiz shows such as *The Missing Link* and *Mastermind* are current examples in the UK. In this case, then, it is not so much an oppressive context that may exert power over students, but an unexamined taken-for-granted assumption about learning that arises from a general experience of the practices of schooling, that themselves were undertaken with no choice but to engage in them.

Ramsden's, Svensson's and Saljo's work add to our picture of the student experience by showing how the student's perception of the pedagogic context influences the approach that a student is likely to adopt. There is thus an interaction between the student's personal and psychological context (orientations to learning, prior experience, conceptions of learning) and the task demands and particular pedagogic context which influence the approach adopted by the student. Entwistle (1997: 4) summarises the negative consequences of this interaction in the following way:

> . . . much of our current teaching and assessment seems to induce a passive, reproductive form of learning which is contrary to the aims of teachers themselves.

However, Morgan and Beaty (1997) indicate through a longitudinal study of Open University students the positive aspects of higher education as students seem to develop more meaning focused conceptions and approaches to learning over time. They also signal the importance of the development for the student of confidence, competence and a greater sense of control over their own learning. They argue that confidence is necessary for the development of competence, and that this then allows the student greater responsibility for their own learning.

The hope held out by the research presented in *The Experience of Learning* is that we can enhance the positive aspects of the higher education experience (as indicated by Morgan and Beaty for example) by attempting to influence student approaches to learning by changing task demands and pedagogic contexts. Marton and Saljo (1997) however warn that it is much easier to induce surface approaches than to create contexts which require deep approaches.

Three trends can be discerned in research which has built on the *Experience of Learning* tradition. The first is a move towards quantitative research that uses study strategy inventories of various kinds in order to investigate relationships between psychological and pedagogical factors and learning outcomes (Entwistle et al., 1979; Entwistle and Ramsden, 1983; Ramsden, 1992; Biggs, 2003; Entwistle and McCune, 2004; Vermunt, 2005; Heikkilä and Lonka, 2006). Despite differences between these inventories, three approaches to study tend to be apparent across all – a meaning orientation (associated with a deep approach), a reproducing orientation (associated with a surface approach) and an achieving orientation (associated with a strategic approach) (Entwistle and McCune, 2004: 330), and the findings from these studies tend to support a positive relationship between meaning or achieving oriented approaches with successful study outcomes (Vermunt, 2005; Heikkilä and Lonka, 2006).

The second trend is relevant to our understanding of the student's psychological context of learning and concerns acknowledgement of the significance of the student's metacognitive capacities for their success in learning and the inclusion of self-regulation as a key concept in student learning research (McCune and Hounsell, 2005; Vermunt, 2005; Heikkilä and Lonka, 2006). For example, McCune and Hounsell (2005: 257) expand the concept of a 'deep' approach to learning to include 'systematic, well-organised, self-regulated studying', and the development of 'ways of thinking and practising' appropriate to the discipline. In doing so, they rename the deep approach 'high quality learning'.

The third trend informs and elaborates our understanding of pedagogic context in understanding student approaches to learning and study success. This is exemplified most forcefully by a recent Economic and Social Research Council research programme, the Enhancing Teaching-Learning Environments in Undergraduate Courses (ETL) Project (Anderson and Day, 2005; Entwistle, 2005; McCune and Hounsell, 2005). This research builds on the existing assumption in the *Experience of Learning* tradition that the effect of context on student learning has to be understood as mediated by the student's perceptions of the teaching-learning environment (Entwistle, 2005: 4). It also builds on Biggs' systemic view of the teaching and learning environment encapsulated in the concept of 'constructive alignment' (2003). Biggs combines student learning research with constructivist perspectives in the field of cognitive psychology to propose the need for curricula which align teaching and learning activities and assessment with intended higher order learning outcomes in such a way that students are necessarily drawn into active and productive learning processes. The ETL project seeks to understand this alignment through an investigation of student perceptions of different teaching-learning environments in different disciplines and how these are seen to support – or not – student attainment of 'ways of thinking and practising' in the discipline (McCune and Hounsell, 2005: 256). In this project, the pedagogic context has been enlarged to include the wider context of external professional bodies, national subject benchmarking, and employers' expectations, as well as institutional quality assurance processes, resource distribution and the different value given to research and teaching in different institutions (Entwistle, 2005). McCune and Hounsell (2005) also emphasise the context of the disciplinary community with its particular norms, language and practices, and Anderson and Day (2005) emphasise the complex, dynamic and temporal nature of context as a 'threading' of different interacting factors such as cultural and technical tools, goals, norms, practices, prior experiences and institutional structures. We can see in this elaboration a shift from the purely pedagogic context of earlier research towards a more socially informed conceptualisation of context which takes account of the social, institutional and disciplinary situatedness of teaching and learning. What is still missing from this account of context are the effects of power within this. I explore and develop this in Chapter 4.

The research reviewed in this chapter has made a significant contribution to our understanding of the student learning experience by highlighting the *situated* and *relational* nature of learning in higher education from what students tell us about their experience. It has demonstrated how the student's approach to learning and studying, and hence their experience of learning, emerges out of an interaction between the student's own psychological context and the particular pedagogic context they are in – what Prosser and Trigwell describe as the student's learning *situation* (1999: 13–14). And more recent research has begun to elaborate the nature and scope of this context. The research also implicitly points to features of the pedagogic context which suggest themselves as significant for understanding the effects of power on study and student learning – assessment, workload, opportunities for student choice, support for learning, disciplinary norms and practices, and institutional structures, values and regulations. And Saljo's work hints at the significance on students of their prior experience of schooling and the wider context of societal assumptions about what learning is.

Effects of power, whilst not directly addressed by these studies, are relevant to understanding the accounts of the student experience offered here. A perspective which takes account of power highlights the fact that studying is not a natural or a neutral process, but a practice that arises when a person places themselves within an institutional context in order to learn and within which their learning will be judged and accredited accordingly. Such a relationship between the individual and the institution cannot help but invoke relations of power. It is these relations and their effects which are part of the ways in which higher education enables or limits the student's capacity to engage meaningfully and productively in their learning experience.

The purpose of the next chapter is to enlarge this view of the student experience by shifting the focus from 'how do students go about learning and what influences this?' to 'what do students say about their experience of higher education and what does this tell us about what is experienced as enabling or as oppressive?'

3
The experience of being a student

There is often a silence at the heart of teaching. This is the silence of the students' and the teacher's experience as the class unfolds and as the students go about their daily business. What fills the silence are the requirements, instructions, announcements and questions of the teacher and the curriculum, and the students' responses to these. In order to get closer to the ways in which power may be at work in the learning context, we have to get behind the noise and busy-ness of the classroom and the curriculum to reach the silence beyond.

> If we had a keen vision and feeling of all ordinary human life, it would be like hearing the grass grow and the squirrel's heart beat, and we should die of that roar which lies on the other side of silence.
>
> George Eliot

We have to get close to the roar that lies on the other side of the silence of the classroom and the daily lives of students, for it is only in that roar that we can begin to develop an understanding of the lived experience of individuals within the higher education context.

The recent National Student Surveys (NSS) in the UK and Yorke and Longden's survey of the first-year student experience (2007) suggest that many students express satisfaction with their study experience. And Yorke and Longden conclude that the first-year student experience is generally a good one (2007: 43). Areas of dissatisfaction identified through the NSS are to do with assessment and feedback, and with course organisation and management. Whereas the first year students surveyed identify making friends, good teaching and learning experiences and the development of independence as some of the best features of their experience, they identify managing time and workload pressures, poor feedback, isolation and poor teaching as some of the worst features (Yorke and Longden, 2007). Such conclusions offer a promising picture of the student experience.

As I said in Chapter 1, it nevertheless obscures the fact that some respondents to the NSS will have found their experience to be unsatisfactory, the picture of the variation in experience between students, across time, and within different teaching and learning contexts is obscured, and 43.5% of possible respondents did not respond. As Prosser (2005) argues it is important to read such surveys as indicators which have to be further contextualised in the specifics of the different learning environments experienced and in the range of responses given to any one item.

Although there may be commonalities amongst individuals, the biography and past experience of any individual means that their lived experience of any event will be particular to them. Each individual's account of their experience is significant, for it offers a window into the multiplicity of experience, enriching our understanding of humanity and 'enlarging our thinking' (Arendt, in Barr and Griffiths, 2004: 88). In the context of education, such a focus allows insight into the richness and particularity of student experience, whilst at the same time ensuring that such experience is not lost to silence. Given my concern in this book to examine the workings of power in the institution and how a student's experience can be disabling or enabling, the concern with individual experience in this chapter is essentially to bear witness to the different accounts students offer of this. Such accounts contribute to the hermeneutic aspect of critical social science – the foregrounding of the presentation and interpretation of subjective experience as a starting point for critical social analysis.

This chapter presents a patchwork of brief accounts from a selection of student voices taken from qualitative studies published in recent years and from unpublished data collected through an evaluation interview, a focus group and a learning journal in my own work context.[14] This is not an exhaustive selection. The picture presented is inevitably partial. It is limited by the particular historical, social and cultural contexts of the studies selected and by the particular students involved. The studies draw on a range by date of publication from 2002 to 2007. Although most are from the UK, Australia, Canada, Finland, Holland, New Zealand, South Africa, Spain and the USA are also represented, as are the range of disciplines. Whilst most of the studies focus on undergraduates, some include graduates and taught postgraduates, with direct entry as well as mature and non-traditional students. The studies I have concentrated on include those I have noted as interesting and those identified through a recent literature search using the terms 'student', 'experience', 'student perspective', 'engagement', 'alienation' and 'higher education'. I have also focused on qualitative studies where it is possible to read the words of the student speaking about their experience. More detailed information about these studies is summarised in the table in the Appendix at the end of the book in order to give the reader a feel for the contexts within which the original data was collected.

In each section below, I begin by quoting from student comments as they appear in the research literature.[15] I follow this with a brief elaboration of the issues which seem to emerge from these accounts. The title of each section tries to capture the key themes expressed. In this way I build up a patchwork of the student experience, each quotation a different piece added to create a pattern which says something about the engaging or alienating aspects of this experience. Whilst the individual's situated experience is lost in this process, an overall picture may emerge from the gathered scraps.

One way to read these voices is as a basis from which to theorise the student experience. Such a reading requires attention to their reliability and their validity as representative evidence to inform such a project. An alternative reading of these voices is to engage one's emotional self and simply 'listen' to what is expressed, to hear what is evoked and what it says of human experience in the context of attempting the project of learning in a higher education institution. Drawing on Barthes (2000), Archer describes this second kind of reading as the 'punctum' in opposition to the more rational 'studium'.

> I would describe the 'studium' of the text as the dry, intellectualised readings produced at the level of rationality. In contrast, the 'punctum' represents the emotional engagement between reader and text, the 'felt' experience . . .
>
> (Archer, 2004: 465)

I invite the reader to explore the student experience in higher education through a 'punctum' reading of the following student voices. Parts 2 and 3 of the book offer its 'studium'.

The student experience

Struggle and privilege

> I registered with the agency and sometimes for two or three weeks they won't even call me and there is no other wages coming in. When I don't have money and the bills are coming in and sometimes I find it difficult to pay to the school, I can't read, the pressure piles up on me, I can't study. It really gets me down. (mature male student)
>
> (Moreau and Leathwood, 2006a: 32–3)

> I really don't know how they expect you to do the reading . . . I've got to work three nights a week and then I've got to cook three nights a week, I know this is just me personally, and I've got family responsibilities as well. I don't know how they think people are able to do all the stuff. (female student)
>
> (Moreau and Leathwood, 2006a: 35)

> Yes, I live with my parents. They pay for my books and everything. Obviously I've got my loan now and I don't need to pay rent or electricity and all that. I just pay for my travel. I should be all right for a year. My parents aren't poor. (female student)
>
> (Moreau and Leathwood, 2006a: 36)

I can't get back to get my little girl after school. Now I pay excessively for the childcare service. Classes that are late I can't do . . . I've had to see lecturers more about asking for extensions and they are never very forthcoming and it's got nothing to do with disability. I've got a child, I get her to bed, I sleep with her from 8.00–10.00 p.m. and I set an alarm and get up and work till two at night . . . I don't believe in the assessment system. I know it's meant to be fair assessment and everyone's got the same chance, but that's rubbish. Some of my friends are out working every hour God will send. Others, their parents pay for everything. (mature single mother with a physical impairment)

(Riddell et al., 2005: 639)

The money situation is going to be hard but it's either this or I work in a shop for the rest of my life. (female, 21, criminal justice)

(Guest and Bloomfield, 2004)

My parents are going to support me financially. They'll pay for my accommodation and things like that, and they'll bail me out when I need it. I don't really expect to be in debt when I finish the course. (female, 18, history)

(Guest and Bloomfield, 2004)

She [room mate] doesn't work. She – her parents pay for everything. She's lazy. I work my butt off. I don't know. It teaches me more discipline, because I have to manage my time. It's like, okay, I have to work, so I have to do my homework before I go to work. And then she's like, 'Oh, I'll do my homework tomorrow' kind of thing. I don't have that time, you know. (female student, withdraws)

(Bergerson, 2007: 108)

I had a violent relationship with my husband and that stripped my self-confidence and dignity and assertiveness and while I'm on this course I am trying to rebuild those things and that is my main issue. (first-year student)

(Kimura et al., 2006: 76)

The whole of the first semester was a nightmare from beginning to end . . . things were finally in place . . . six or seven weeks in. By that point I was behind . . . I hadn't done any work, and for obvious reasons it takes me longer to write an essay than most people. (blind student)

(Goode, 2007: 46)

These comments reveal the different circumstances from which students engage in higher education. For some, parental financial support and freedom from responsibility lead to a roomier, more carefree experience. For others, poverty, family responsibilities, disability, and a desire for a better future lead to the need for part-time work, pressured study time, loss of play, time juggling, and inhibiting stress. Whilst higher education holds out the hope of significant improvement in life chances, this comes at a cost financially. These differences seem to rest on the extent to which privilege or its lack influences the students' starting position in higher education.

The emotional roller-coaster of studying

... there used to be times when I felt really down and I just got on the phone to [my mum] and cried and said how much I hate being here ...
(Wilcox et al., 2005: 713)

You don't know who you are going to live with ... I was so scared, it was like going into the Big Brother house or something.
(Wilcox et al., 2005: 714)

A lot of your self-esteem is derived through your ability to be successful and your ability to do a good job, and when you feel that you're failing that's a huge issue, a huge issue. (mature student with dyslexia)
(Riddell et al., 2005: 638)

It affects me in the sense that, for example, if I've made a great effort in that subject and I fail, my morale will be at rock bottom. You may start asking if you are any good as a student ... Yes, it really affects me, above all when I feel like finishing my studies, just like now.
(Llamas, 2006: 680)

It was just, it was like, the truth. Like the Bible or something. It was such a revelation I just couldn't believe it. I couldn't believe society was like it, but it totally made sense.
(Lambert and Parker, 2006: 478)

Sorry for crying during our conversation. I didn't expect that I would have to recall some of the memories I didn't want to recall, at least not now. Despite the hard part, I do consider this year [to be] one of the most precious phases of my life and I do learn a great deal in different perspectives, say, both from culture shock and learning shock. (female overseas student)
(Griffiths et al., 2005: 284)

Someone spoke to me today in lecture – which was very exciting. We are meeting on Thursday ... So inspired after lecture that I headed back to the library to study some more. The view out of the window was the main part of the university – it was very fulfilling; and I realised it was worth it after all. (first-year mature female, arts, from journal entry week three, term three)

These quotes reveal the pleasures and pain of studying. It is embodied and shot through with feeling – excitement, fear, revelation, inspiration, anxiety, loss of confidence, hatefulness, stress, disengagement, dread. There is a dynamic emotional texture to these accounts which reveals the processual nature of being a student. It is not a static state but a state of flux.

Self-confidence seems crucial in this, and can be gained and easily lost. Seemingly small things can make all the difference – making a new friend, who you are going to live with, the anticipation of a mark, or seeing something differently. Fragility of self-confidence and the ups and downs of the learning experience seem to make these students susceptible to being undermined by things going wrong in relationships, communication, assessment and general circumstances.

Engaging experiences – people and processes

Gaining confidence

> She fills you with confidence. When I had my exam results and stuff, I mean they're OK but I wasn't that pleased with them and she's still like, 'Well, you've done pretty well'.
>
> (Wilcox et al., 2005: 716)

> I began to feel that I believed in myself, that I didn't want to remain in second place, I wanted to study and get the master's degree. (female accounting student)
>
> (Moore, 2006: 157)

Tutor recognition and respect

> Yes, my course leaders are *so* positive helpful and friendly.
>
> (Clegg et al., 2006: 107, original emphasis)

> My tutor always listens to and values what I have to say but he is also critical in a way which doesn't make you feel stupid.
>
> (Tett, 2004: 6)

> 'That's the first one you've missed'. That guy [tutor] didn't know me from Adam. I felt good about that, pulled me up. It was wintertime. I wanted to pack it up. (first-year mature male, arts, interview)

Collaborative inquiry

> The fact that we all knew we had to do it [a collaborative real-life problem-based learning project], and that there was no way it would be done if only a few participated, drove us all to perform as well as we could. The fact that the students were given total responsibility for the project gave us even more of a boost as we knew this would reflect on us all personally.
>
> (Harland, 2002: 8)

... one of the bigger strengths is [faculty] didn't allow – and I would say the students didn't either – there to be any interdisciplinary barriers, they just broke the barriers down all over the place ... (social work student on interprofessional course)

(O'Neill and Wyness, 2005: 437)

... Everyone sits around in a circle and you have discussions and bring up subjects and your voice is just as important as the teachers, and everybody has as much credibility as each other. ... You know your teacher and the teacher knows you, that adds a whole new dimension to it. (female, creative arts)

(White, 2006: 244)

Problem-based tasks

He would come and then give us a question on the board and we'll all do it and he'll be walking around and he'll be asking you, 'why do you write [this] here' and you actually have to explain to him. ... So we'll all have a chance to look at it, do it by yourself, before he does it on the board, rather than [the lecturer] coming with the example and doing it on the board and we'll all think 'oh yes we do understand' and then when we have to do it, we see that that 'eh heh, I actually didn't understand a thing'.

(Case, 2007: 131)

Facilitation

You [tutor] were there for us if we needed you but you did not force upon us what seemed right to you.

(Harland, 2002: 12)

Lecturers are people who come and, they just give information, they don't care that you understand ... but he's different because, ja I think he cares that you get what he's saying, even if you're in a tutorial you call him, you explain to him, he actually listens to what you don't understand and then he'll explain to you, in any way that you'll understand.

(Case, 2007: 131)

Getting to know others

... they broke us up randomly otherwise you'll just choose someone that you know. And I was with two people that I never even met before and yeah. Well now I know them really, really well.

(Case, 2005: 18)

Just recently I've started to go out with them [friends on my course] actually through the group work which is quite good . . . so that's given me a few new friends just from doing that project . . .

(Wilcox et al., 2005: 717)

I found it, Sheffield's been very, very, very, you know supportive, in our department cos our department's, our department's kind of different, in to really anything, cos it's so, it's like a little community in itself, and everybody's, erm, you know, kind of close . . . (first generation male student)

(Dibben, 2006: 99)

Peer support and discussion

Because we were there on the first day and helped each other out really, not so scary . . .

(Clegg et al., 2006: 106)

The problem was that everyone had their own ideas on how the case study should be presented hence only the more vocal people making the decisions. But we soon realized that this wasn't going to get us nowhere. So we went round the group one by one and listened to what each member had to say. This was a success as we penned out a plan on who would present what area of the case study.

(Burke and Dunn, 2006: 228)

Personally meaningful assessment

It [journal] gives people a structure, not to cling to, but to negotiate with. (male design student)

(Barrow, 2006: 369)

These quotations give a feel for how things can be when things are going well. They express the pleasure of experiencing a new confidence and the hope this gives for the future. They reveal the satisfaction of taking responsibility for working independently or cooperatively to achieve a genuine task and experiencing competition with others as productive within the context of cooperative group work. There is enjoyment from meeting and working with students from other cultures and backgrounds and the significance of peer support, for example when learning and understanding can be enhanced by talking things through with one's peers. Also significant seems to be the necessity of a certain kind of present but non-intrusive tutor support and the positive power of realising that your tutor knows who you are. Allied to this, friendly and encouraging tutors who can challenge and explain without diminishment and a sense of departmental community are other positive factors.

Four themes seem to be particularly important in supporting student engagement and the opening up of learning – the opportunity provided by structured activities to go beyond normal ways of being and doing; the significance of tutor support and recognition; feeling respected as an adult and as a human being; and the opportunity to talk with peers. All of these reveal the productive and positive effects of the institutional context in the educational process – through curriculum design, interpersonal relationships and communication.

In the next section I present accounts of the harsher, alienated aspects of the student experience.

Alienating experiences

Lonely

> . . . Because you do feel really lonely and I think that really plays on your mind, so that you feel so bad . . .
>
> (Wilcox et al., 2005: 713)

> A big part of me wants to pack it in, but my pride won't let me! I wanted this so much – to be able to study at X – and I'm trying to hold on to that. However, I haven't really made any friends and feel very isolated, so it is difficult to judge how good/bad my progress is, as I have nothing to judge it against. (first-year mature female, arts, week five, term one journal entry)

These quotations indicate the experience for some students of being isolated in a crowd. It is as if in some contexts the co-location of geography, architecture and social organisation produce an impersonal and anonymous context which can disorient and overwhelm the student, leaving them feeling lonely, isolated and not supported.

An impersonal and uncaring social milieu

> The feedback consisted of a circled grid, and the lecturer had not engaged with her ideas at all. There were very few written comments at all. The student had experienced a great sense of 'let down' as she had been so interested in the topic.
>
> (Hutchings, 2006: 256)

> My personal tutor, I wasn't particularly impressed with, in that he intimidated a little and I don't, I felt that he didn't particularly listen . . .
>
> (Wilcox et al., 2005: 717)

I was expecting something in the post beforehand . . . (mature male chemistry student)

(Harrison, 2006: 380)

The class sizes were really big and so they didn't have much time anyway and then even when I did manage to get time to speak to [lecturing staff], they didn't really seem that interested. (male electronic engineering student)

(Harrison, 2006: 381–2)

At university you have large groups, lots of people in one lecture. At college there are only about 25 people and you all get to know each other. The lecturer knows you. Everything is fine. Here the lecturer doesn't even know if you walk past him. He doesn't even know if you are a student. It makes it hard.

(Thomas and Quinn, 2007: 91)

In tutorials, it's crowded and it's like crowded emotionally as well. Because you're thinking, like, this is my only chance to talk. (honours student, arts, focus group)

Sometimes I have the feeling that they [teachers] find it difficult when you ask a question, not all of them, but some. . . . They do not look up and they just continue their story and if he's ready he's ready. Maybe he does not know the answer. (male student)

(Severiens et al., 2006: 83)

[I want lecturers to] not be there because they're there for their research – and lecturing is just a second part to what they do. Because a lot of them are there for research and some of them don't actually care what they are saying. (female, arts)

(White, 2006: 237)

These comments express the distance that some students feel between themselves and academic staff. This is compounded for some where they feel not listened to or crowded out by large numbers of other students. At its worst this is experienced as a cold, impersonal, hierarchical and formal social environment, creating a distancing and excluding effect. Recent research by Lee and Rice on the international student experience in the USA suggests that one of the difficulties international students have to negotiate are social relationships both within the institution and within its local social context that can be excluding and even at times derogatory and confrontational. Lee and Rice also suggest that such social distancing and hostility is most likely to be experienced by students from non-Western and non-English speaking backgrounds (2007: 405). In the UK context, Gill (2007) identifies tutor support and encouragement as significant in the adaptation of Chinese students to the UK higher education context. Lack of this, and worse, implied criticism such as '[you] shouldn't have come on the course', make the experience of such students very difficult (2007: 174).

Competitiveness between students

I assumed we would use all the tools we found here to get these things [job, career]. But the course soon became a competition, like high school. People trying to impress, as if they were competing for prizes. They showed a lot of selfish interest in the course but not in the other students. This was the first shock. (male overseas business student)

(Griffiths et al., 2005: 286)

Everybody thinks only of themselves. Many classmates refuse to lend you their class notes . . . besides the higher marks you get, the better it is for your curriculum vitae, and so they trample on the others. (female social work student)

(Llamas, 2006: 673)

I felt that if I said anything I would get shouted down. The atmosphere was aggressive, aggressive, aggressive. Most of the aggression came from one person and was directed at me. There was competition between us. (female business student)

(Griffiths et al., 2005: 288)

These students express their dismay or disappointment at the experience of a competitive and in some cases aggressive ethos in which self-interest in the pursuit of marks dominates.

The despotism of time and workload

A bewildering amount of stuff first year students had to absorb and learn. I had to hit the street running. If I had stumbled I don't think I would have got up again (first-year mature male, arts, interview)

. . . and I did the whole thing again, and then I realised, no, time was running out, so then I went on to this [question]. . . . It was just like there was no time for the paper.

(Marshall and Case, 2005: 264)

I think the year's going really fast, I feel there is extra reading that I should be doing, it's getting too much and I feel that I'm not really in control.

(Clegg et al., 2006: 108)

But then again you realize that reading is an inefficient way of learning when you are under so much time pressure.

(Griffiths et al., 2005: 282)

The students here seem to be overwhelmed by work, by 'stuff', and by the speed of everything. They seem to feel unable to give time to slower forms of study like reading. It is a question of working at speed and feeling an inability to complete or give time to extra work. There is no space to pursue their own agenda and no space to pause or 'fall'. Keeping up means getting by and not giving time to engaging deeply in their studies. Not keeping up leads to a feeling of a loss of control.

According to Hounsell (1997: 255) the experience of time pressure and heavy workload is borne out by research which shows that lecturers misjudge how much time an assignment will take students by about two thirds. This suggests that students may be having to go at a pace that to them is at least two-thirds faster than lecturers assume they are going.

Doing time[16]

> If the teacher is explaining something and I don't agree, I keep quiet. All I want is to finish quickly and go home, so I don't waste my time getting involved in the class.
>
> (Llamas, 2006: 673)

> To me, London was a very depressing city. My life there was nothing but school, library, computer room, and my flat. The only entertainment I had in London was shopping at the supermarket. . . . Every day I had to put an invisible facial mask on before walking into the classroom. (overseas female business student)
>
> (Griffiths et al., 2005: 285)

> Others just drone on and you think, 'Oh, yes, what are we on about now?' And you listen and there's just nothing there. There's nothing to actually spark you to get you motivated.
>
> (Gale, 2002: 69)

And Case (2007: 123) describes the dominant experience of chemistry engineering students on one course as one of 'non-stop academic work' requiring self-discipline and drudgery with no experience of enjoyment, 'no fun', leading to the experience of fulfilment from the completion of work or to disengagement and a loss of motivation.

The students in this section seem to experience studying as something that they are not in control of, where the work or commitment required is experienced as threatening or boring, and limiting. For some this means simply giving time to sitting there so that they might just absorb something – what Gale calls 'tests of time' (2002: 68); to others it seems to mean discipline and denial, and the negation of their own social and inquisitive selves. Either way, study appears to involve compliance to the requirements of others, leading to a focus on getting through the course and passing exams.

Compliance, consumption and reproduction

> Very often, work at university is not a search for the truth or the right way to go, but a search for what the relevant teacher will assume as 'right' or 'true' and this is something I always had difficulties dealing with.
>
> (Harland, 2002: 12)

> We all know of injustice and bad manners everywhere but nobody complains, nobody says anything about it. (psychology)
>
> (Llamas, 2006: 679)

> In my class nobody has ever been opposed to the teacher, I mean overtly in front of them. Later in the coffee-shop, everybody talks about what is OK and what is not to their way of thinking. (education)
>
> (Llamas, 2006: 673)

> We don't make any suggestions or questions to the teacher . . . we just let them go on with their explanations because we feel like running out of the class. The sooner, the better. Let them waffle, we write it down and that's it. (engineering)
>
> (Llamas, 2006: 681)

> I do take into consideration what [lecturers] think, but I basically go about my own way of doing things and if they don't like that, well that's their bad luck. (female, arts)
>
> (White, 2006: 241)

> The thing is customers will trust you better in the long run if you've got a piece of paper, that's the way I'm seeing it . . . there's always ways to, there always seems to be people can sort of ask to get the answers off or something like. People have sat the test before and they sort of got their results back, what not. . . . There's generally the same group every exam so you just take turns of going first just sort of on a roster basis, it's all set up. (male student)
>
> (Kitto and Saltmarsh, 2007: 163)

> Anyone can open the book, copy the formula, write it down. So many assessments for those kind of courses are actually assessing something which is not the application, is just copying. . . . OK yeah – learn the formula, copy that down – excellent. And then you get an A or something and you still do not know what it does. (male business student)
>
> (Barrow, 2006: 361–2)

Here the tone expressed is one of compliance to what students assume is required of them in the academic learning process and passivity in the face of teacher authority and what might be experienced as unjust or discourteous. The focus is on getting by, by noting what the teacher says (for future reference or examination), and not rocking the boat. Resistance is expressed outside class and through engaging in learning by playing the academic study game.

Control

> What can I say?!! Feel like I'm slipping deeper and deeper into unfamiliar waters – actually, more like walking accidentally into sinking sand! Had great difficulty following lecture. A couple of times we were to discuss x with neighbours . . . both my neighbours were with friends so I ended up feeling very isolated and quite overwhelmed by the lack of knowledge I seem to be equipped with. (first-year mature female, arts, week four, term one journal entry)

> I think there is something about the whole Honours thing that is a bit freaky actually . . . I mean I said that I came here to enjoy, which I did and I have been. But there is so much pressure, and there is such a feeling of . . . You know, you are so close and yet you know, you might not get there. . . . but I met a girl yesterday who is in fourth year and she says it's just an everyday feeling, that sort of feeling in the pit of your stomach when you think you are going to be sick . . . (honours student, arts, focus group)

> There's no resources I can go to; there's no notes that came with the lecturers' books . . . When I can't get information for skipping a lecture, I find that very frustrating. . . . The learning is not in my court anymore; it's him [lecturer] trying to control how I learn. (male, science)
> (White, 2006: 238)

Here the students seem to be expressing concerns over a lack of control over their learning brought about by not understanding, not knowing, not being able to access resources, the amount of material to cover in the time available, or the fear of the perceived arbitrariness of exams – being so close to passing and yet so far from doing so. In the case of not knowing or not understanding, there seems to be a feeling of not being able to act in order to work on what needs to be understood in a way that will help to gain a hold on it. Where there is a feeling of being overwhelmed by speed and amount of material, the same issue arises. Students feel not in control and therefore unable to act on the material in a way that will help them to learn. It is as if students are arrested and rendered unable to act in ways that would be most helpful to them.

The honours student quotation is slightly different. It is not so much that the student is 'arrested', but rather the prospect of sitting exams which are perceived to depend on 'things going well on the day', is sometimes literally sickening. Here the issue is one of the student not being in control of the means by which they can best demonstrate their achievement and capabilities.

Mystified, challenged and confused

I went to a philosophy lecture and this woman said, 'Is my hand raised, or is it a figment of your imagination?' I went home and burst into tears. I was eighteen, and that kind of general conceptual, as well as procedural, confusion stayed with me the first three or four months in the first year.

(Haggis, 2002: 213)

Told another tutor [about not getting feedback on an essay except 'didn't answer the question']. You should have done something about it [said the tutor]. I didn't like that. What about responsibility on the other side? Between you, me and the wall, but I can see that was right, it was my responsibility. It is my right to be told, but if I don't assert my right, I'll sit and do what I've done – most people – all my life. (first-year mature male, arts, interview)

I gave up at the end of December going to practicals because there was simply no point. I would sit there looking at a computer and just think 'Oh my god, what's going on?' (male engineering student)

(Harrison, 2006: 381)

. . . is like finding yourself suddenly, wake up in a completely different place, it felt so strange: different expectations, different course organisations, different modes of study, you name it, everything is different. This is the third week, and I am still disoriented. I am also stressed out, and feel that I am making very little progress (Chinese postgraduate student)

(Gill, 2007: 172)

These experiences of confusion may potentially ultimately be positive, but seem to be experienced initially as either very upsetting or unsettling, or as quite exciting, whilst others are simply unhelpful. This theme of confusion runs through the following section in relation to the issue of language.

Another language

Violet: . . . Because when he's giving the lecture and he's like talking, talking, talking, saying those words and things. I said my God, I don't know what you saying! I'm lost! [laughter]

Paula: I think that's another culture shock in a sense, the language. It is a different language, from being at college, from being at school. It is a totally different language. (black mature Caribbean students)

(Read et al., 2003: 271)

Learning for Gary *unfortunately* entails text as a necessity. He views the academic process as being closely tied with *difficult* reading. As a dyslexic learner he finds his relationship with text an acrimonious one and sees text as the enemy, something completely unrelated and distant from himself.

(Greasley and Ashworth, 2007: 835, original emphasis)

. . . learning is time-consuming, because reading is a slow grind . . .

(Greasley and Ashworth, 2007: 835)

My experience during the first week on the course was very painful. I was knocked down by my poor English. I couldn't understand what the lecturers said and found it impossible to follow the case studies. I understood about 10–20%. In group discussions, there was nothing I could say. My confidence and self-esteem collapsed. (overseas business student)

(Griffiths et al., 2005: 290)

The particular issues here are the unfamiliarity of academic discourse in general, the difficulty of reading for a dyslexic student, *and* the particular difficulty of working in a foreign language. For the students, there seems to be an issue of how to get hold of the language and to work out the meaning of what is being said.

The quotations in this section suggest the possibility that students experience the engagement with academic discourse – either in their own language or in another – as one which positions them as an outsider, as not fluent, and which in the process dispossesses them of their own vernacular tongue and preferred modes of communication.

Intellectual diminishment

Fear of appearing to be stupid:

And I'd think 'if they ask me . . .', and I was always crouching down . . . And I would sit at the front in the front rows . . . and I was scared and. . . . And I was mostly embarrassed cos of the people . . . cos of my classmates. For the lecturers no, because the lecturers what could they do? Ask a question, and sometimes you know the answer and other times you don't. Me, it was mostly because of the other students. (male working class student)

(Rosado and David, 2006: 358)

Cast as stupid:

Whenever I go talk to molecular biology professors, they make me feel, I don't know – he's a nice teacher, but they make me feel stupid. . . . I couldn't even divide ten thousand by ten – I was so nervous. One time he said 'did you understand what I just said?' I said 'uh-huh', so he said 'repeat in your own words,' and I couldn't. (female molecular biology student)

(Johnson, 2007: 815)

Mostly it's my classmates they think I am stupid, and I got most frustrations from my classmates in class. That made me did not want to go to class before. . . . (Did you feel frustrated when you were misunderstood as a stupid person?) Yeah, and I could not get into their groups, and I was so quiet, and I was isolated, and that made me feel uncomfortable and hurt and unhappy, and I didn't want to go to the class. . . . Because in that whole process, I did not contribute anything. I mean I could, but I couldn't in that group. . . . I am not stupid; that's important for them to understand me . . . I am quiet does not mean that I am stupid. I am quiet does not mean my opinion is not valuable. And I need respect from people, and it's very important for them to listen to me, have some patience to listen to people. That's it. (female overseas student)

(Hsieh, 2007: 5)

Choosing where to sit to avoid feeling stupid:

You're not a drifter [if you're sitting in the middle]. You're not up the back and you're not down the front, you don't know everything . . . If I sit down the front I feel stupid because I'm not the brightest of people, and they've already got all the answers. Up the back they don't want to know the answers so you sit in the middle and usually in the middle there are people who are trying to find out what's going on.

(Gale, 2002: 72–3)

Cast back to being a 'stupid' school boy:

If a tutor re my opinion, says 'don't go there', it will translate in my head into 'you stupid boy, sit up straight', back to school. I didn't like school. (first-year mature male, arts, interview)

Silenced for fear of the consequences:

She says that she is afraid to voice her own opinion because of possible repercussions from the lecturer.

(Hutchings, 2006: 254)

Has a fear that reader will think she doesn't understand.

(Hutchings, 2006: 257)

A significant issue for some students is the fear of being seen to be stupid and thus diminished in their own and others' eyes. This fear seems to arise in the context of the evaluative relationship between teachers and students, and students and students, implicitly at the heart of an educational process founded on assessment. In this context, asking for help, asking for extensions, choosing where to sit, or whether to speak or not become fraught with the possibility of being unkindly judged as stupid. Particular circumstances can also prompt this fear. For example, when perceiving other students to be more intelligent or knowledgeable than oneself, or experiencing tutor interventions as a reprimand to be silent in the way this was experienced at school. The consequences of this fear of being stupid are significant and disabling for they seem to result in a withdrawal from participation, from seeking help and clarification, and in keeping quiet and losing concentration. These consequences have the potential to undermine some students' sense of their own efficacy and in doing so threaten their integrity and self-confidence. Other students on the other hand may respond by perceiving the threat of diminishment as a challenge.

Being different

Out of place:

> The environment itself is different, the way you learn is different, the way the classes themselves are structured is different. . . . Not feeling accepted maybe, on a hall, you may be the only black person on a whole hall where people are trying to get to know each other but that's one more label that you may have to you know, counteract against other people in your hall who may not be as open or may not be as accepting to other people who are not like them, on the, on the level. So, I would say in the housing communities, in the classrooms, at social events, that would be the main weariness and you know uncomfortability when it comes to you know, freshman coming in. Especially minority students.
>
> (McClure, 2006: 1047)

> I'm very suspicious of people making a judgement about who you are depending on whether you tick a box or you don't. Because I think people don't understand that you can have dyslexia and be a completely, perfectly affable, perfectly bright person who just has a few problems in these areas over here.
>
> (Riddell et al., 2005: 638)

> So at the end of that course I started meeting more deaf people and I started learning sign language and that was a kind of a real epiphany, it was amazing and it was the first time that I could really express myself and just chat in a group and the first time that I really started having complete access to an academic environment. So that was a very positive experience.
>
> (Riddell et al., 2005: 639–40)

And so a lot of times I felt out of place, because you see all white faces.

You know I'm the only fly in the buttermilk, so that took some getting used to . . .

(Davis et al., 2004: 420)

A chair that was too small 'told' a student that she was 'older, fatter, and not the typical student', especially compared to the others, who seemed not to fill up their chairs.

(McClelland et al., 2002: 5)

My values and attitudes to life are different – quite often I sit in the corner doing my own thing whilst the others are doing lots of things together and sometimes I feel isolated although haven't focused on this coz I don't have time to waste socialising. (first-year mature student)

(Kimura et al., 2006: 69)

Having to do better:

I'm always on my Ps and Qs and know that I've got to do better than anybody else. I have to. And I'm not sure that that's, you know, absolutely true in somebody else's eyes, but just the situations I've been in and the way people have treated me, it makes me feel like Oh, I have to do better than best for them to see what I'm really capable of doing, what I'm really, really capable of doing.

(Davis et al., 2004: 432–3)

Hyper-visible:

Because in most of my classes when we talk about an issue that deals with black people I become like the black representative of the United States of America.

(Davis et al., 2004: 435)

Invisible:

And I can remember some of my classes, going into some of my classes, not really being recognized because I would raise my hand and it would be like I wasn't there. I didn't really understand that, because I know people see me. I know I'm not invisible.

(Davis et al., 2004: 436)

We become invisible in the classroom in the Western academy due to our communication differences. For example, as Arisaka (2000) points out, in Japanese society where the majority of the people speak softly and pay enough attention to others, one is visible enough. But, here in the West, we get labelled as 'submissive and quiet'.

(Mayuzumi et al., 2007: 589)

Silenced:

There was a clique against me; eventually this clique made all the decisions and just informed the others by email . . . If I go to a meeting now, I don't say anything. (male overseas business student)

(Griffiths et al., 2005: 286)

What I noticed is that some Chinese students will give their opinion when asked. But when they are challenged, they can't back it up, and then they withdraw into themselves. After that it is as if they have lost all opinions. We [now speaking as a 'Chinese person'] like to voice our opinion, but not to be confronted. (female overseas business student)

(Griffiths et al., 2005: 289)

I also have an experience of feeling negated and humiliated by a professor. When I didn't understand his lecture in a political science course, which was a requirement for my undergrad degree, I went to ask him desperately for some help. Instead of trying to understand my circumstance, he interrupted me and just said, 'Go back to ESL class' as if it was simply my fault because of my poor English skills. He did not question his way of speaking in his lecture, which was mumbling, or consider my unfamiliarity with US politics. Then, I felt something was not right and I was feeling sad and humiliated. But, I was not sure what was wrong in the situation. Consequently, I was losing self-confidence and motivation to study. The professor did not give me any space for me to talk, but silenced me. (female Japanese student)

(Mayuzumi et al., 2007: 585)

Like if I say something about my experience back home if the whole class just, there was nothing to say. Well, I start a bad thing, right? People are not interested at all or they don't see the connection, so they just start something else to discuss . . . Then the instructor says okay and the whole class moves on to other stuff, very smoothly for them, I think. (female Chinese student)

(Zhou et al., 2005: 300)

I didn't feel comfortable in the group, really sharing my ideas, so therefore I didn't. I was just sort of silenced. And I found out when I did speak about things, it wasn't really acknowledge . . . (social work student on interprofessional course)

(O'Neill and Wyness, 2005: 436)

Is this my place?:

It was my first sociology lesson, I went and sat there, it was a small lecture room, what were we? – about 30 people there. I looked around and thought: genius, genius, genius, genius, genius, what am I doing here? (mature female student)

(Moore, 2006: 155)

And, you know, you, no-one forces anything, you know, you don't have to, no-one says 'oh, tell me, like, what your background is' or whatever, I mean, it's just like more easy going. It's like you know, it's like starting afresh, it's like a different life here, like, from home, you can kind of cut off, and you know, you've got, your uni life is, your uni life. (male third-year first generation student)

(Dibben, 2006: 107)

Juggling:

It's like two people, my ethnicity doesn't affect university as such but I have to have two lives, one as an Asian mum and one as a student. (final year female)

(Kimura et al., 2006: 70)

These students feel different from the dominant culture of the institution they are studying in. Such differences can be of culture, skin colour, nationality, class, family expectations, gender, sexuality, language, physical capabilities, size and age. The experience of difference arises from the collision between their own particular circumstances and the assumed or experienced institutional norm of the student as young, full-time, white, able-bodied, and middle class. The experience of difference seems to combine feelings of standing out, being looked at, feeling at odds with, marginal to, invisible in, silenced, spoken on behalf of or speaking in another language, and made an object of study or impatience. To these students, their hold on the institution can therefore feel precarious, as if they are at the institution under false pretences. Such experience can lead to feelings of isolation, unfairness, frustration, anger, and low self-esteem (see for example, Davis et al., 2004: 427–30).

These feelings and social positioning out of the institutionally constructed mainstream can have powerful effects on the individual. These are produced through the naturalisation of an implicit social norm, expressed through social relations, practices, and assumptions, which privileges a particular 'type' of student as universal. However, as one student with dyslexia asserts, no one student is a type. In a world of 'mongrel identities',[17] the different complex and changing aspects of identity necessarily mean that most students will at different times in their life in the institution experience feelings of being 'out of it' and not belonging, and this is most likely to occur in the first year when the culture of the institution will be at its most unfamiliar. But there is no necessary relationship between the social structural position one holds and one's experience as a student. For some students – whatever their background – the intellectual challenges that higher education offers provides an exciting and liberating experience that opens up new horizons of understanding and being.

Commodified and objectified

We're learning to accept mental bondage and the social and economic subjugation which is going to be imposed on us later in our lives. I want people to ask themselves: Whose interest is it serving to write all these essays? What impact are our studies going to have on us? Are they going to liberate us, or just have us scraping our claws in the dust and trying to grind out a living, so we can work a nine hour day, come home, watch Eastenders and fall asleep?

(Campus Celebrity Enigma, 2002: 6)

. . . because I feel factory-farmed. I am an educational bulimic. They make me binge and purge all of this knowledge without any time to absorb or digest it, and I think to be truly student centred you have to make a space for the individual in that and the way the system currently works there isn't the space for us as individual people. (final year, mature female)

(Lea et al., 2003: 328)

These two comments vividly express a feeling of being rendered into a product or commodity by an educational system which is seen to give no time and space for the individual and which simply fulfils the need to produce employees for the wider economic system. In these students' eyes, being a student means complying with the control exerted by the requirements of institutional study, which rather than free students to critique, challenge and change the system, projects them as future passive workers.

Summary

This 'punctum' of student voices provides some insight into the experience of being a student in higher education. It is offered as a subjective enrichment to the personally stripped out accounts of the student experience offered by student learning research. The quotations indicate how, whilst at its best, higher education can really engage the student in an enjoyable, rewarding and meaningful learning experience, it may also produce the often silent alienation that can lie behind the noise of the busy daily life of the 'classroom'. When the student is engaged productively in the learning process they seem to feel confident, respected and acknowledged. They work autonomously and cooperatively with other students on inquiry driven projects in which they extend and reframe their understanding.[18] They value the opportunity to talk things through with each other, feel supported by tutors and peers but are themselves also supportive of others. In this way, they take responsibility for themselves and for each other.

When the student is alienated from the learning process they may feel lonely, bored, confused, silenced, fearful of being seen to be stupid, invisible, or much too visible. Their activity focuses on getting things done that are required by others, at a pace and volume that is often counterproductive to their learning. There is a feeling of not being in control and of needing or choosing to play 'the game' in order to succeed under these conditions. Academic staff are experienced as distant and impersonal, and academic discourse as an alien language. This alienation seems to be the product of a range of institutional conditions including privilege, social isolation, impersonality, hierarchical social relations, workload, assessment, academic discourse, a culture of expertise, the production of difference, and the preparation of students for the labour market.

The student voices presented thus highlight both the potential and the wasted opportunity of the higher education experience. The purpose of the rest of this book is to try to understand why this experience arises, and to go beyond an explanation that is founded on the relationship between individual student differences, their psychological context and pedagogic practices to a consideration of the role of the institution itself as a context for learning.

Part 2

The institution as a context for learning

Whilst getting close to individual student experience through different student voices allows us to envision what is significant for students and how it may affect their actions, it is not the whole story. Individuals do not stand alone. Subjective experience is not hermetic. It arises through interaction between the individual and others in a historically constituted cultural, social and political world.

Broadly, educational research is concerned with the investigation of a phenomenon – learning – when it is situated within the particular context of the educational institution. In the case of higher education, this is the institution of the university. Higher education is not a natural phenomenon. It is a historical practice which has evolved over time, shaped by multiple political, economic, cultural and social forces. My argument in the second part of the book is that if we disregard the social formation of higher education in understanding the student experience, we risk being blind to the significance of power in the educational process and in the experience of the individual student.

According to Morrow and Torres (2002: 22), the key contribution that Hegel makes is the argument that the capacities to know, reason and be autonomous cannot be seen as socially or historically given. That is, reason, knowing and autonomy cannot be seen to be unchanging, ideal forms available in a pure and essential way to individuals, somehow untouched by history and society. Instead, these capacities need to be seen as constructed within and by a dynamic social and historical context which includes struggle for mutual recognition between individuals or groups who are in relations of domination to each other (Morrow and Torres, 2002: 22). These themes of history, society and power were then built on by Marx who argued that how individuals experience and act in the world will be determined by the social and historical conditions produced by differences in power based on the organisation and control of capital within society (2002: 22). The argument in this book is that in order to understand the experience and actions of students, we need to examine the particular social and institutional conditions within which this experience and action takes place. This is the contribution made by the 'analytic social knowledge' aspect of a critical social science as discussed in Chapter 1.

In the second part of the book I therefore examine the particular social and historical context that the institution of higher education provides for the student experience and investigate the workings of power within this. In doing this, I offer a critical analysis of the role of the institution in the student experience. Chapter 4 develops a framework for understanding the institution as a context for learning, identifying key aspects highlighted by such a framing. Subsequent chapters address these at the macro socio-economic level, at the institutional level and at the micro level of the immediate context. I argue that in any one instance of study, it is necessary to understand how the student engages with and experiences study from the perspective of the immediate context of the interaction between the individual and the task they are undertaking, and also from the perspective of the wider institutional and socio-economic contexts which inter-penetrate this immediate context. Chapter 5 thus deals with the economic and social functions of higher education, and Chapter 6 with the institutionalisation of time, space and activity and its effects on the self. Chapters 7 and 8 then address the discursive nature of learning tasks in the institution and the special case of assessment.

4
Context and power

In this chapter I develop a framework for analysing key factors that are significant in thinking of the institution as a context for learning. I then summarise different conceptions of power and discuss how these might operate within the institutional context. I begin by exploring what I mean by context.

The institution as context

Context can self-evidently mean that which surrounds us in any particular setting. Within language, context can include what surrounds a text, or phrase, or word, and enables us to make sense of it. For example, we can make sense of 'it' in the last sentence by referring back to 'a text, or phrase, or word' and realise that it substitutes for these. Or we can make sense of a sign above a shop not just in terms of the text itself but also in terms of its location above the shop, the type of shop itself, where the shop is and so on.

Sitting here writing, the context in which I am doing this appears to be simply the room I am in, the time of day, the fading winter light outside my window over the fields, the fact that the heating is on and I am warm and that I have just had a cup of tea. I am alone in the house, writing using the keyboard and screen of my computer, referring to articles or books, and to some kind of plan I have in my head for what I want to achieve today. I am also aware of the fact that my husband will be home soon and we will need to negotiate things like unpacking the shopping and making a meal. Other aspects of the context include the fact that I am writing a particular kind of text – a chapter in an academic book – and I need to be mindful of the social, academic and discursive conventions which govern what is appropriate and legitimate to write, in what style, and so on, in this kind of text. I am also conscious that I am writing for a reader who will need to understand what I am writing and who may also evaluate what I am writing according to these conventions, their own interests, and ways of viewing the world. While writing I am therefore sometimes conscious of others and their view of me, and the implication of this for my sense of self and my identity as an academic and writer. My sense of self and my writing are also bound up with how I locate myself within the discipline or academic community I belong to and in relation to the university I work for. While writing I am therefore implicated in particular relationships of mutual expectation, responsibility and accountability within these communities. How I interpret these conventions, identities, social relations and obligations, and the significance I attach to them, forms part of the context within which I write and may therefore affect how I experience and approach this task.

Seven characteristics of context can be inferred from this description.

1. To understand the meaning of something – whether text, an object, an activity or an experience – we need to understand it in relation to its context. Understanding student experience means interpreting it within its context.
2. An immediate description of context is likely to be external and physical – what I see or am aware of through my senses. In other words, the self-evident, vernacular experience of context – what we assume context to be – is what we see, feel, and hear around us, including who we are with. It is our construction of the material context – what surrounds us in time and space. It might also include our current experience of time and its relationship to what we are doing – whether we have a sense of unbounded time or of limited time, a sense of flow or of pressure.
3. In addition, this material context includes the tools and technology that mediate our discursive and other activity, and in so doing enable and constrain these in particular ways. In my case, these tools currently include a laptop computer, word processing software, a bibliographic database, a memory stick, a printer, access to the Internet, pens and paper, books, articles and so on.
4. On closer inspection, context can also include the invisible and immaterial but present internal or mental world we inhabit and bring to any experience or activity – our plans, desires, feelings, beliefs, values and attitudes concerning what we are doing and who we are with. This internal world is shaped by biography, experience and current life situation, and frames the construction of what is significant and meaningful at any one time for the individual in the particular context in which they are in.[19]
5. Whilst in the context I have described I may at present be on my own, I am nevertheless referring to my husband in my head and more importantly addressing an imagined reader through my writing. Although solitary activity may appear superficially to be non-social, it almost inevitably involves an implicit social relationship with others. For example, a student is likely to bring assumptions about the relationship between themselves, what they write and their potential reader to the activity of

essay-writing. Given that their reader is likely to be judging their text and thus judging them, this implicit social context is likely to be particularly significant to the student's sense of self and their own capacities and identity as a student, and perhaps even as a son or daughter. Context always entails social relations, even if at first glance it does not appear to do so, and this aspect is especially potent within the educational context.

6. The activity I am undertaking, in this case writing, is not somehow innocent and primeval. It is cultural. It is something that other humans across different cultures and societies have undertaken in the past, are currently undertaking and will continue to do so. It is a social and discursive practice that has developed over time to take on different forms, values, and conventions. There are different kinds of writing. The different texts produced – and their authors and readers – are valued differently in different contexts. And each of these different forms of writing is governed by different rules and conventions. The extent to which I have access to and am fluent in the production of text according to these conventions will influence my success as a writer and therefore form part of my context as a writer. It is not only the activity of writing, and other discursive practices, that are cultural.[20] All the other dimensions I have identified (time, space, material context, tools and technology, the individual subject, social relations, and activities) also need to be understood as culturally constituted and constructed. For example, our experience and use of time in the West is founded on a particular calendar and on particular assumptions about what constitutes the length of a working day, amongst other things. And this experience and practice may vary across different cultures and for different individuals, depending on their own particular biography and how it intersects with the particular local, institutional and societal cultures they are part of. All human activity, including cognition, is necessarily realised and constructed through social and discursive practices that have emerged over time within particular societies, social groups, institutions, and local communities.

7. The contextual dimensions I have identified – space and time, material, technological, individual, social and discursive – could be said to be present in any immediate context of activity as affordances and restrictions on what the individual does, and emerge at the intersection between the individual, the material and the social. And significantly, these dimensions and the relationships between them change as the individual moves through time, space and activity. Like a snail and its shell, individuals are never without context. As Lave and Wenger (1991) put it, 'there is no activity that is not situated.'

In seeking to understand the student experience as either empowered or oppressed, my aim is to uncover those aspects of context that are often overlooked in psycho-pedagogic accounts. In other words, those aspects associated with the fact that learning in higher education takes place within an institutional context which is itself part of a wider societal context. In what follows I offer a conceptualisation of the institution as a context for learning. Figure 4.1 maps this conceptualisation and how contextual layers at the cultural, institutional and local levels may enmesh the individual and their activity in particular ways of being and doing.[21]

Figure 4.1 summarises the view that in order to understand a student's experience and academic activity, we need to understand it as something that is situated within an immediate context, within the context of the institution, and within the wider cultural and societal context. The immediate context tells us something about the specifics of who is involved in the particular activity, when, where, doing what and how. The institutional context tells us that this activity is taking place within the context of higher education with its particular economic and social functions, its conventional ways of

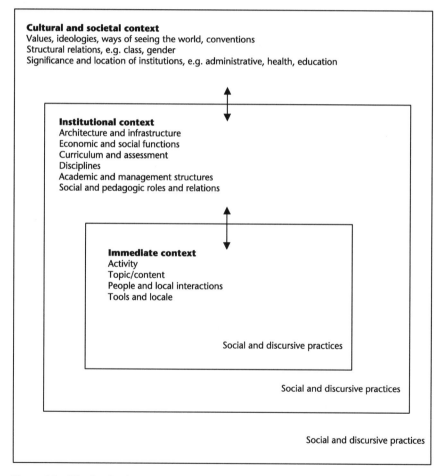

Figure 4.1   The institution as a context for learning

organising, communicating and validating knowledge through the disciplines, curricula and assessment, its academic and management structures, its social and pedagogic roles and relations, and its physical space and infrastructure. And that each of these features of the institutional context will be instantiated in particular ways within different individual institutions of higher education.

Figure 4.1 further tells us that the activity under question not only needs to be understood in terms of its immediate context and its particular and generic institutional context, but also within its wider cultural and societal context. This wider context makes its presence felt through the particular values and ways of seeing the world that individual participants bring to the activity in question, the particular social conventions that govern appropriate behaviour and interaction between people in the wider society, and through the social and economic structural relations which lie behind the interactions pursued. For example, an individual student's participation in a seminar may be influenced not only by the particular social relations they have with the other students in the group and with the lecturer, but also by their understanding of what is expected of a student and a lecturer in a seminar, and by their understanding of appropriate forms of address and turn-taking for example, in more general social interaction. Context therefore needs to be understood as an interpenetration and interplay of factors from the wider social context, the institutional context, and the immediate local context. And, as Figure 4.1 indicates, these factors are realised at each level through particular social and discursive practices. Thus, whilst at any one time the specific characteristics of the participants of any one interaction, and the background cultural norms, values and assumptions they bring with them from their own biography, will form part of the context, this context will also be shaped by institutional practices and the wider societal ones.

I do not wish to suggest by this that contextual factors either have a causal determinate effect on the actions and interactions of participants – a determinist position. And neither do I want to define context only as perceived and experienced by participants, such that individual perception is seen to have a determinate effect on action and interaction – a subjectivist position. I want to suggest that it is both. In other words, that there is a dialectical relationship between subjective construction of context (an aspect of agency) and external social, material and institutional conditions (structure).[22] The double-headed arrows on Figure 4.1 aim to emphasise this point. Although we may say that any immediate context will be influenced by the wider institutional context, which itself will be influenced by the wider cultural and societal context, it is also the case that local activity can shape wider institutional culture and practices, which may then in their turn influence the wider context beyond the institution. For example, discussions that take place within a Masters seminar group of university teachers may be influenced by the institutional conventions that govern the practice of seminars and by wider social values concerning how adults of a certain age may address each other. And yet these discussions themselves may influence participants to challenge such institutional conventions through changes in practice which might have societal effects through the influence these changes have on their students over time.

Whilst our individual experience, and interpretation of that experience, would seem to be what determines our actions, there are nevertheless real material and economic factors that influence our capacity to participate in and contribute to particular experiences and activities. There are real social structures that differentiate between individual human beings, privileging some over others. And there are real norms, conventions, taken-for-granted assumptions and discourses that exist prior to any one individual and which govern what are appropriate and valid social and academic practices. To participate, one has to enter into this prior order, but this prior order and one's access to it is differentially structured. In this way, context can be said to constrain our actions and interactions.

We are not however passive participants. We have the capacity to reflect on ourselves and our situation, and to act on ourselves, with and on each other and our environment, and in this way to transform it and ourselves. We are therefore in a dialectical relationship with context. Context shapes us, our actions maintain or transform context, which then further shapes us, and so on. In this way, we are our context, we produce our context in negotiation with others, and context also has real effects on us. The perspective presented here thus combines a subjectivist and a realist position through a dialectic between individual agency founded on an individual's interpretation of what is significant at any one moment and an external social, cultural, economic and material world which has effects on this interpretation and agency.[23]

Such a framing of context hints at the different ways in which power might work within the dialectic of agency and structure: '. . . all human action is carried on by knowledgeable agents who both construct the social world through their action, but yet whose action is also conditioned or constrained by the very world of their creation' (Giddens). Or in Marx's words: 'Men make history, but not in circumstances of their own choosing' (Chouliaraki and Fairclough, 1999: 97).

This account of context has sought to redress the omission of power in accounts of the student experience by highlighting the social nature of being a student and the societal and institutional setting of this learning experience.[24] In the following section I discuss the different ways in which power might be seen to operate within the university context of higher education.

The institution and the exercise of power

I here outline two different conceptions of power – sovereign power and distributed power, and show how each can contribute to our understanding of the workings of power within the context of higher education.

A sovereign view of power

We can think of power in a number of ways. A simple starting point is to think of power as something that an individual has by virtue of their position, their personality, the weapon that they hold, their wealth and so on, and which enables this person to get others to do what s/he wants, or to inhibit others from doing what they want.

> Power as a locus of will, as a supreme agency to which other wills would bend, as prohibitory . . . In short, power as negation of the power of others.
>
> (Clegg, 1989: 9)

Politically, one could associate such a view of power with a figure such as Mao Tse Tung or Louis XIV. More prosaically, one could imagine such power operating in the classroom through the capacity the lecturer has to direct the actions of students by virtue of the lecturer's role. Essentially, the dynamic captured here is the capacity of a particular agent to direct and thus reduce the agency of others. Callon and Latour describe this as a process of 'translation' which seems particularly apt when applied to the educational context:

> The means whereby an actor [teacher] translates the 'voice' . . . of other actors [students] into passive voice, with the privilege of active voice being captured by the translator.
>
> (Callon and Latour, 1981, in Clegg, 1989: 27)

Where the curriculum is organised in such a way that prescribes what students are to do, how and when, we can say that the curriculum, as instantiated by a teacher, translates the students' agency into a passive voice. Such passivisation can have an effect on the student's capacity to act, their choice of action to undertake, their sense of self as an agent, and thus on their emotional resilience and health. This translation from active to passive voice thus constrains the student's autonomy and the capacity to take responsibility.

So far this account of agentive power has focused on individuals – the agency of one individual to limit the agency of others. We can however develop this view by substituting for the individual agent particular social groups with particular power interests, for example a capitalist class exercising power over other classes, or men in a patriarchal society exercising power over women. From this perspective power can be said to operate in order to maintain the interests of a particular group by limiting, undermining or re-directing the interests and capacities of other groups. Whilst such dominance and coercion might arise through obvious means such as military or physical force, legislation serving the interests of business and capitalism, and/or unequal distribution of wealth necessitating the majority to work for a wage or salary, the question arises as to how it is possible for such power relations to be maintained. Why do oppressed groups not rebel against such dominance? Gramsci (1971) offers an explanation. According to Gramsci, the dominant class maintains its position through the oppressed class's consent to this. This consent is achieved through hegemony, '. . . the naturalisation of practices and their social relations as well as relations between practices, as *matters of common sense . . .*' (Chouliaraki and Fairclough, 1999: 24, my emphasis).

These practices and social relations are naturalised through particular social institutions that maintain and reproduce the dominant culture – 'schools, media, family, political parties' (Eagleton, 1994). According to a Marxist point of view, the only way for a socialist revolution to take place is for 'organic' intellectuals to 'organise the cultural life of the people' thus producing a 'counter-hegemony' (Eagleton, 1994). This conception of the naturalisation of the common-sense world as 'truth' in such a way that masks how such common sense operates to support the maintenance of power relations in society is also associated with the concept of 'ideology' (Chouliaraki and Fairclough, 1999: 24). Both 'ideology' and 'hegemony' are proposed as powerful indirect means of maintaining the dominance of a capitalist class.

> It is the supreme exercise of power to get another or others *to have the desires you want them to have . . .* to secure their compliance by controlling their thoughts and desires.
>
> (Lukes, 1974, in Clegg, 1989: 3, my emphasis)

Clegg (1989: 4) argues, after Foucault, that all three of these conceptions of power – individual power, class power, and subtle hegemonic forms of class power – constitute a 'sovereign' view of power which emphasises agency and a causal relationship between this agency and its effects on others. The fundamental premise here is that the effects of power can be traced back to an originary agent – one who exercises sovereign power – in whose interests it is to maintain and reproduce existing power relations. This originary agent could be an individual or a social class and the means of exercising power can be direct and obvious, or more often indirect, invisible, and through particular institutions.

A distributed view of power

A very different view – associated with Foucault – challenges the originary view of sovereign power and argues that there is no 'decisive centre of power' (Clegg, 1989: 7). Instead, the way that power operates in the modern world is a result of the management of populations rather than domination of individuals (Fairclough, 1992: 50). In any particular immediate context then, power cannot be reduced to any one person or dominant group, but power is always present.

Power is implicit within everyday social practices which are pervasively distributed at every level in all domains of social life, and are constantly engaged in . . .

(Fairclough, 1992: 50)

In his investigation of power in society, Foucault (1980) emphasises an inescapable relationship between knowledge and power and offers three different ways of understanding how power operates. These are via discourse and discursive practices (Foucault, 1972), via disciplinary practices and bio-power (Foucault, 1979), and via technologies of the self (Foucault, 1988). I discuss each of these below.

In his earlier work, Foucault (1972) was concerned with the ways in which discourse constitutes social life through rules that govern what we take to be appropriate knowledge. In other words, how the conceptual frameworks we use in order to make sense of the world, what we assume our subjectivity to mean and how we should therefore relate to each other, are all embedded in and produced through discourse and discursive practices (Fairclough, 1992: 39–42). A key point, especially in the social sciences, is that what we might take to be a 'natural' and 'objective' phenomenon such as 'learning', is in fact formed within particular discourse(s), for example psychological and educational ones, which are themselves historically produced. Learning is therefore not something out there, it is generated through discourse. This constitutive characteristic of discourse highlights the significance of discourse as a form of power – the power to construct reality in particular ways. It contains both a negative understanding of power in discourse as creating realities that support the interests of powerful groups (as in hegemony and within ideologies) but also a positive understanding of power whereby agents have the capacity through discourse to transform such realities. Given that Foucault is working from the premise of a distributed and non-originary perspective on power, it is important to note that he sees any particular interaction or discursive event as an *intermingling* of discourses, allowing for the possibility of flow, opposition and resistance within discourse:

> There is not, on the one side, a discourse of power, and opposite it, another discourse that runs counter to it. Discourses are tactical elements or blocks operating in the field of force relations; there can exist different and even contradictory discourses within the same strategy; they can, on the contrary, circulate without changing their form from one strategy to another, opposing strategy.
>
> (Foucault, 1981, in Fairclough, 1992: 59)

Foucault (1979) develops a disciplinary view of power in his classic text *Discipline and Punish – The Birth of the Prison*. In this work, he describes power as operating through concrete practices or *'micro-techniques'* associated with institutions such as medicine, prisons, and schools, whose roles are to manage the health, behaviour and capacities of populations. An example of such a technique is the 'examination'. The observational and assessment processes involved in examination (either medical or educational) render the individual visible through judgements based on statistically derived norms of behaviour. Through this process of evaluation the individual can be located within a hierarchy in relation to others who have been similarly examined. According to Foucault, such techniques illustrate the inseparability of power and knowledge in modern societies (Rabinow, 1991). For example, although a 'technique' such as learning styles inventories may have developed as a result of social scientific theory and research with the aim ostensibly to contribute to our understanding and enhancement of learning, in actuality the practice of using such a technique can act as a form of power creating a particular normative way of thinking about learning which the individual can be measured against. In this way, forms of identity, cognition, normality and deviance are produced. Power/knowledge can therefore be seen to be productive in the sense that techniques of power *produce* subjectivities which are suited to a world in which such techniques and disciplinary practices operate. Foucault terms this form of power 'bio-power' because it is concerned with the measurement and analysis of human life at the level of populations, and which in doing so, transforms it. Echoing a hegemonic or ideological critique of power, Foucault asserts that power 'is tolerable only on condition that it masks a substantial part of itself. Its success is proportional to its ability to hide its own mechanisms' (Foucault, 1981, in Fairclough, 1992: 50).

In his later work, Foucault is concerned with ethics – the ways in which the individual acts on the self in such a way that the individual self constitutes himself or herself as a moral subject, 'that is, the way they "conduct themselves" and "bring themselves" (*se conduire*) to obey (or disobey) a set of prescriptions' (Foucault, 1988, in O'Leary, 2002: 11). The means by which such subjectivities are produced are described as 'technologies of the self', for example 'confession', 'self-examination', and 'care of the self' (O'Leary, 2002: 33, 47).

This view of power is relevant in the present discussion in the sense that it suggests that any individual is never free to constitute themselves as they wish. The technologies of the self available to us are culturally and historically bound and associated with the different expectations on us given our biographies and particular social positions. A young probationary lecturer is nowadays usually expected to engage in reflective practice on their teaching in order to complete any required training and, thereby, pass through probation. A student is required to develop 'self-awareness' as a learner in order to monitor and plan their progress through personal development planning. These are examples of the recent introduction of confessional technologies of the self into higher education. As noted earlier, such technologies are productive in the sense that they create particular subjectivities. They are loci of power forming the individual in a particular way. And they are embedded within multiple practices and technologies of the self from different domains. They can also be resisted or transformed.

Gore (1993: 55) argues that taken together, the constitutive power of discourse, the disciplinary micro-techniques embedded in day to day practices, and technologies of the self form what Foucault (1980) terms 'regimes of truth' – what we take to be true, the means by which we establish truth, how we should behave in our search for truth, and who is able to sanction what will count as truth. The important point is that, whilst such regimes of truth govern our ways of being, our social and discursive practices and our fields of knowledge, they are not 'true' in the sense of being natural, absolute and universal. They are historically, culturally, and socially constructed and are not traceable, according to Foucault, back to a particular originating creator. They are therefore also contestable and subject to transformation.

Power and context

In this account of sovereign and distributed power I have tried to highlight six different ways in which power – as part of context – might operate within any one particular activity or interaction. These different forms of power are summarised in Table 4.1.

A number of conclusions can be drawn from this account of different forms of power about the inter-relationship between power and context in higher education:

- Power is present in all contexts of activity in higher education. We can therefore describe context as a 'field of power relations' (Foucault, 1991: 247).

Table 4.1 Forms of power

Sovereign power	Distributed power
Originary	Circulatory, multiple
Power of an individual over other individuals The capacity of an individual to determine the actions or experiences of others	Discourse formations Constitutive of what counts as knowledge, subjectivity and social relations
Power of a class or social group over other groups The capacity of a social group to determine the actions of other groups	Disciplinary practices and bio-power Practices which render the subject visible, examinable, calculable and available to be judged
Hegemony and ideology Naturalisation of power relations as common sense in order to produce consent to these	Technologies of the self The action of the self on the self through engagement in particular practices

- Universities are centrally implicated in relations of power in society as they are concerned with the production and legitimation of knowledge through research and assessment, and the advanced formation of professionals and graduates through teaching. They are thus involved in the production of 'truth' and in the formation of subjectivities which contribute to the maintenance and reproduction of the economic and social functions of higher education in society.
- Power can be experienced as a concrete presence within relations between members of the institution, for example through the directive requirements of teachers on students.
- Power can be felt indirectly through the ways in which the access different people have to different material and social resources will either facilitate or inhibit their engagement with particular activities. For example, a female student who has limited masculine middle-class cultural resources to draw on may be disadvantaged within a higher education context in which masculine middle-class cultural values and norms dominate.
- Power is rendered invisible through the naturalisation of particular ways of thinking and acting which favour the interests of dominant classes, as if they were simply common sense. For example, the widely held view amongst academics that some students do not have the intellectual competence to succeed has quite different consequences for students compared with the view that higher education is delivered and organised in such a way that renders some students unable to succeed.
- Whilst power may reside in an individual by virtue of their position as teacher, the particular dynamics of any one interaction may involve a shift and flux in the flow of power within the group, between teacher and students, and students and students.
- Teachers do not straightforwardly control students, though the practice of assessment gives highly significant power to the institution through the role of the academic teacher. Students also hold power within the educational encounter. Shifts in educational discourse and practices from student as learner to student as 'client' or 'consumer' reframes the teacher-student relationship, putting greater pressure on teachers through emphasis on public accountability, student evaluations of teaching, and threats of litigation.
- The taken-for-granted study activities of higher education – lectures, seminars, exams, essays, learning journals, labs – are practices which constitute techniques of power and technologies of the self that constrain and may produce particular subjectivities of both teachers and students.
- Social, discursive and disciplinary practices, social and pedagogic relations, and the organisation of the curriculum – including assessment – together form a specific academic culture or 'regime of truth' which require particular ways of being, acting and interacting on the part of teachers and students.

- Whilst such interactions are framed within academic culture, such culture is also itself subject to, and influences, the discourses and ideologies, and the economic and social relations within the wider society.
- A dialectical account of the relationship between agency and structure assumes that power operates through both in such a way that involves mutual influence and thus transformation of each over time.

My purpose in offering this analysis of context and power has been to show how any experience is inseparable from context, how power is always implicated within context, and how any investigation of the student experience needs to locate this within the institution as a specific context in which power operates in such a way that may enable or limit the individual student.

My purpose has also been to show the different ways in which power can be conceptualised and to indicate that these different forms of power operate at the different levels of context identified in Figure 4.1. In other words at the macro societal level, at the institutional level, and at the micro level of the immediate context. By including a sovereign perspective on power I uphold the possibility that any one individual can feel the limiting or enabling effect of another individual or social group upon them, for example within local interactions or through tasks required. And such a perspective also implies that it is important to be mindful of the ways in which particular *interests* are served by the current organisation and institutions of modern society, including higher education. Giddens reminds us that whilst capitalism is a key institution shaping society, three other institutions representing powerful interests are also significant – industrialism, surveillance and state violence, and each presents us with particular problems:

> . . . the gap between rich and poor accentuated by contemporary capitalism, the destructive impact of industry on ecosystems, the repression of human rights in the context of intensified surveillance, and the threat of a major war.
>
> (Chouliaraki and Fairclough: 1999: 79)

Whilst it is important to consider how particular effects of power serve particular interests, I have also drawn on the distributed view of power because of the emphasis it gives to the ever-present workings of power in any situation. It also allows account to be taken of the multiplicity of interests that may be operating at any one time in any situation, for example those of different disciplines each with their own regimes of truth. And the Foucauldian perspective on modern society as disciplinary allows for the examination of higher education practices as productive of regimes of truth governing the subjectivities of students and teachers, and what it is to learn, know, and produce knowledge.

In what follows, I explore the 'field of power relations' in higher education by focusing on four different, though related, aspects of the institution as a context for learning. In Chapter 5, I address the economic and social functions of higher education. In Chapter 6, I examine the institutionalisation of time, space, activity and the self. I then investigate the particular social and discursive practices required of students in higher education in Chapter 7. And in Chapter 8, I discuss the special case of assessment.

5

The economic and social functions of higher education

In this chapter I explore the consequences of the current focus on higher education as a means to contribute to the economic wealth of society and the concomitant emphasis on the production of student employability. I also examine the function of higher education in the maintenance and reproduction of social relations. In doing both these things, I tackle the ways in which wider societal imperatives intersect with the institutional context and thus impact on the daily lives, practices and experiences of students, and their teachers.

The economic function of higher education

Higher education has changed significantly in the last twenty years or so. It has grown in size through the number of institutions offering graduate level education and through the numbers of students who now enter into such programmes.[25] Earlier changes in the UK, heralded by the Robbins report in the early sixties, whilst calling for access to higher education for all who were capable of making use of it, did so in a climate of increasing public funding, the principle of no upfront fees, and the provision of maintenance grants. Whilst the aim was to thus enhance the skills base and economic performance of the country and thus indirectly the benefiting of society, it still held as an implicit value the intrinsic worth of higher education and the importance of academic freedom. More recent changes and policy initiatives (for example the Dearing report and the 2004 Higher Education Act in the UK), whilst still centred on further increasing provision and access, have done so in a context of funding constraints, stricter accountability measures, the legitimation of the raising of income through fees, and the loss of maintenance grants. Such changes have also firmly positioned higher education in the policy discourse as having a central role in producing graduates who can contribute to the economic health and wealth of the nation. This has contributed to the 'marketisation' of higher education and the 'commodification of academic knowledge' through the appropriation of academic discourse (Ainley, 2003: 350).[26] At the same time, more and more young people are said to be seeking higher education for the purpose of certification and its 'exchange' value in the employment market (Ainley, 2003: 34). Furthermore the 2004 Higher Education Act allows universities (in England and Wales) to set fees for courses according to comparative judgements between similar courses and the success of graduates in employment. In this way, the Act establishes an explicit market in higher education in the UK, with the students as the consumers of universities' products, enabling students to improve higher education provision through consumer power (Tlili and Wright, 2005).

Blake et al. ascribe this economic rationalism to a new managerialism within the context of globalisation:

> Globalization, it is claimed, exacts competitive supremacy in vocational achievement from populations, reductively conceived as workforces. The cost of failure is steep economic decline, and the rights and interests of individuals as citizens, and as autonomous subjects of action and experience, necessarily dwindle, if not vanish in interest and importance.
>
> (Blake et al., 2003: 8)

From this perspective, another reading of 'student' is as 'worker' as well as 'consumer', through what McLaren (2003: 25) describes as the 'capitalization of subjectivity'. In other words, the rendering of subjectivity within education such that it becomes suited to life and work under capitalism. Similarly, according to Schuller, the function of institutionalised learning is the production of human capital and the eventual contribution of the individual graduate to national economic productivity, income generation and self-sufficiency. The foundation of such an education is the epistemological principle of rationality (Schuller, 1999). Schuller contrasts this principle with the generation of social capital through networks and relations of individuals in informal action learning contexts where the aim is the enhancement of the quality of life and relationships, founded on an 'epistemology' of ethics in action. Accordingly, the main purpose of higher education – as an institutionalised form of learning – is the production of rational individuals who can contribute to the economic well-being of the nation.

The distinction made here by Schuller between human capital and social capital can be related to Habermas' distinction between strategic action and communicative action. The former is focused on efficiency and the means to achieving goals, whilst the latter is focused on purpose and values and the attainment of mutual understanding (Morrow and Torres, 2002: 72–3).[27] Habermas also makes a distinction between the 'system' – the world of finance and power (economy and state) – and the 'lifeworld' – the taken-for-granted meanings and values that arise over time through day to day living and communication. Strategic action is associated with the system, communicative action with the lifeworld. The problem for modern society, according to Habermas, is that strategic action has colonised the lifeworld, distorting communicative action in such a way that 'the processes of mediation between system and lifeworld are perceived under imperatives of money and power in functional terms exclusive of communicative interaction' (Rassmussen, 1990: 47). The discourse and rationality of money and power enters and appropriates the discourse and rationality of the lifeworld. The material comes to dominate the symbolic. For example, the production and consumption of oil, legitimated through instrumental means-focused rationality, is pursued despite its detrimental effect on the environment. Asserting the environment as a value over the vested interests of oil requires legitimation through communicative rationality. In this way, system and self-interest could be said to undermine common interests and social value. According to Rassmussen's interpretation of Habermas, the main problem confronting social theory is 'liberation from the consequences of strategic action in the form of the colonization of the lifeworld' (1990: 45). This colonisation essentially distances the lifeworld from the system, and squeezes out the opportunity and space for communicative action which strives for mutual understanding based on social rationality. Whilst in Habermas' view 'the fundamental value that should define social rationality is the reduction of domination through undistorted communication' (Morrow and Torres, 2002: 72), communication becomes distorted and displaced through the incursions of instrumental rationality. The economic function of higher education – an example of strategic action – has the potential to undermine an ideal of social and educational function, at the heart of which would be the 'undistorted communication' of communicative action proposed by Habermas.[28]

From this perspective, one could say that the lifeworld of students and of teachers has become distorted by the system and its related instrumental rationality and discourse, in such a way that leads to the capitalisation of the student as worker or consumer (McLaren, 2003). The massing of students into large lecture halls is an example of a response to requirements on individual departments to increase income by increasing student numbers and to respond to the widening access agenda without a related increase in public funding, which would support the 'undistorted' communicative encounters essential to an education founded on social rationality. In this example, the outcome is both disconnection between students and teachers and a focus on income and outcome. Students and teachers are reduced to elements in a system of production and income generation.[29]

Another example is provided by Dr AW Frank at the University of Calgary:

> In the university, department meetings could, ideally, be a place where communicative action takes place and influence and value-commitments are regenerated. We could, in those meetings, attempt to reach common understandings. In one meeting we were discussing a proposed change to the curriculum. I was trying to ask a colleague why s/he wanted this change; my 'communicative action' involved asking what

s/he was trying to teach, how that teaching was going, and so forth. The colleague's response was: 'If you don't like the change, vote against it.' In other words, s/he didn't want to talk, explain, or reach a common understanding. Instead we would each gather votes and whoever had the most votes would win. Systems media (power, votes) had pushed out lifeworld media (appeals to common value commitments as a basis of influencing colleagues to believe one option or the other best represented who we want to be, as a departmental community). It's important to understand that this colleague acted in a milieu that the university as a system creates: money and power dominate, and local understandings don't count for much. The colleague was part of this colonization process, but s/he was only reflecting a larger process. http://www.ucalgary.ca/~frank/habermas.html (accessed 6 July 2006)

Such an undermining of communicative action in a way that is not obvious and seems natural, is described by Habermas as 'structural violence'.

> The reproductive constraints that instrumentalise a lifeworld without weakening the illusion of its self-sufficiency have to hide, so to speak, in the pores of communicative action. This gives rise to a *structural violence* that, without becoming manifest as such, takes hold of the forms of intersubjectivity of possible understanding.
>
> (Habermas, 1987, in Outhwaite, 1996: 282)

The structural violence wrought by the economic function of higher education has the potential to undermine the ideal function of higher education as offering a quite different kind of public space:

> Despite their failings, universities preserve their importance as examples of communicative rationality and creativity as 'specialized internal public spheres' that carry 'the promissory note of the surprising argument . . . at any moment a new viewpoint may emerge, a new idea appear unexpectedly'
>
> (Habermas, 1989, in Morrow and Torres, 2002: 139)

According to Morrow and Torres (2002: 73) curricula based on instrumental rationality lead to 'non-reflexive learning' – the kind of learning students voice as strategic, or as concerned with just 'getting by', 'privileging egocentric calculation of success' over 'authentic communication' (Habermas 1984, in Halliwell and Mousley, 2003: 89). This strategic approach is aggregative in its effect, rather than transformative of the person and society, and leads to 'self-estrangement', when an individual engages in activities 'that are not rewarding in themselves but are only a means for satisfying other needs' (Seeman, 1983: 179).

It is as if in higher education we have been distracted by the instrumental rationality of means and have forgotten to ask what the values are that we wish to pursue, and to what purpose. If the purpose of higher education was asserted to be – as Ron Barnett (1997) does – one of being able to critically 'read the world' and one's self and others in it, and thus transform it, then such an outcome would be very powerful in contributing to changing relations of domination in society. No wonder then that an instrumentally rational educational system that is non-reflexive and non-critical continues to be prevalent. However, the risk of not examining and taking seriously the analysis of higher education as an institution for instrumental rationality in society, is the perpetuation of 'not-learning':

> Though humans have an inherent capacity to learn in both dimensions [instrumental and social], the tragedy of human history is that *all past and present social formations have distorted the conditions of learning*. As a consequence, for Habermas a theory of social domination is the key to explaining historical failures of 'not-learning'.
>
> (Morrow and Torres, 2002: 73, my emphasis)

For example, Tlili and Wright's research shows how students who enter higher education with the instrumental purpose of improving their employment prospects and who make a financial commitment to this, use employability as a criterion of success. In doing so, they fail to see the communicative potential of education and may replace it with a narrow conception of learning (Tlili and Wright, 2005: 76). In other words, the current social formation which positions higher education as a commodity to be bought and exchanged for future gain limits the individual's potential and capacity to learn.

> Where students perceive themselves as customers, as *receivers* of a service in return for a monetary investment, this undermines the principle that what education 'delivers' should – for well-known pedagogic and psychological reasons – follow from an interactive, cooperative investment of effort and endeavour between teacher and student.
>
> (Tlili and Wright, 2005: 75)

Taylor's (1991) exploration of authenticity provides a way of elaborating this further. He argues that there are three malaises of the modern world. The first is a focus on individualism and a subsequent 'disenchantment' of the world, in which meaning has been lost, as has a concern for and connection with others (Taylor, 1991: 3–10). The second is an emphasis on instrumental reason and a loss of 'ends', which reinforces 'atomism' rather than integrity and purpose (Taylor, 1991: 59). And the third is a disengagement with public political life and with practices of democracy and the issue of freedom.

This opens the danger of a new, specifically modern form of despotism, which Tocqueville (1981) calls 'soft' despotism. It will not be a tyranny of terror and oppression as in the old days. The government will be mild and paternalistic. It may even keep democratic forms, with periodic elections. But in fact, everything will be run by an 'immense tutelary power', over which people will have little control (Taylor, 1991: 9).

Such 'soft' despotism is akin to Habermas' (1973) proposal that capitalism depends on two dynamics. First, operational requirements that are based on exploitation, domination, repression and class segregation, and second, a way of gaining consensus for these requirements through a superficial commitment to democracy, freedom and equal opportunity. Such commitments mask the problems of power inherent in the first requirement, but lead to repeated crises between expectations and actuality (Kearney and Rainwater, 1996: 236).

Similarly, Deleuze and Guattari (1987) propose a tension in the individual between 'revolutionary' desire and 'reactive' desire. The prospects of power, money and status seduce the 'revolutionary' desire away from nonconformity and resistance towards a more repressive 'reactionary' desire to conform to the 'glittering prizes' of capitalism, 'Thus capitalism produces a norm of schizoid *désirants*, desiring machines who acquiesce in their own slavery' (Kearney and Rainwater, 1996: 403).

The slow incremental shift in public discourse and government policy towards a greater economic function for higher education and a focus on performativity produces what Frow (1995: 144–51) terms a 'regime of value' – 'a conformity of cultural judgement and, therefore, to some extent, of cultural experience' (Couldry, 2000: 50), or for Foucault, a 'regime of truth'. Such a perspective becomes self-evidently common sense, and is incorporated bit by bit into university practices through the adoption for example of employability strategies and personal development planning. This 'regime' could be said to constitute a form of 'soft' despotism in which the valuing of individual performance in mass contexts, and of higher education as an instrument of future gain for the individual and society, results in a withdrawal of the individual from participating in the essential question of democracy at the heart of social life, and confusing freedom purely with economic gain – the 'schizoid désirants' of Deleuze and Guattari.

Taylor (1991) argues that the way to confront instrumental rationality is neither to throw it out nor to accept it wholesale, but to engage in public discussion of its value as part of the democratic process, and in doing so, to 'enframe' it within an ethics of care. Essentially, to appropriate instrumentalism to the discourse of care, rather than the other way round. His proposal is linked to his assertion that we must hold onto the value of 'authenticity' as a crucial and freeing aspect of modernity, but in order for this not to collapse into moral relativism, or self-serving self-centredness, its underlying philosophical premises need to be established. These are that we cannot escape our social being, as our identities are forged within social relations, and we cannot escape the 'content' of the horizons of significance of what it is to be human – for example ways of thinking about God, nature, history, society, and so on. But we can express in our own manner (as artists do) our engagement with these key themes. We cannot escape our inheritance, but we can re-interpret it and thus transform it.

Framing higher education within its economic function in society allows us to see how easily this capacity for re-interpretation and transformation within democratic communicative action can be inhibited, and how essential it is for universities to remember the special place they offer society for nurturing the capacity to notice and challenge the creeping and necrotic inertia of 'soft' despotism.

The social function of higher education

Universities express a particular norm of membership, structure and organisation. They are staffed by academics, academic-related staff (administrators, managers, librarians) and other staff (secretarial, janitorial, estates and buildings staff). Academics have a privileged status vis à vis these other staff and in the West are predominantly white, male and middle class. Whilst there are more women academics than previously, these are more likely to occupy junior positions, often part-time. The senior echelons of the academy are still overwhelmingly male.[30] Letherby and Shiels (2001: 130) describe academia as essentially 'a masculine/patriarchal institution' in which a 'hegemonic [heterosexual] masculinity' (drawing on Connell, 1987) dominates, thus subordinating other forms of masculinity and all femininities (see also Lambert and Parker, 2006).

As universities in the UK have increased in number from the ancient Oxbridge, northern and Scottish universities, to the civic universities of the nineteenth century and the plate-glass and new universities of the twentieth century so has the social fabric of the student body little by little spread from the privileged few to encompass large numbers of the middle class; and the gender distribution has changed with female students now approaching 52% of the student population. However, the white middle-class norm still predominates, as does the profile of the 'traditional' student as direct entry from school with the appropriate A levels or highers. 'Non-traditional' students are classed as those who enter higher education through alternative routes, such as through 'Access' courses and who in some ways deviate from the norm.[31] Whilst always open through scholarships, grants and now loans to access by other groups, representation of working-class students and students of diverse racial and ethnic backgrounds therefore continues to be proportionally low. Any student entering the institution from a background that is not middle class or from a family who has no prior experience of university level education may experience marginalisation in this context. Not only do they have to negotiate academic discourse and practices per se, but they usually have to do so within the alien social conventions, assumed world views and practices of the academically successful white middle class. Two concepts are useful here to understand the interaction between individual students and the culture of the institution. These are Bourdieu and Passeron's concepts of 'habitus' and of 'social capital'. Habitus refers to the routine and habitual ways of being and acting in the culture of a particular social group (Bourdieu and Passeron, 1977: 31–2). And social capital expresses the idea that the resources an individual can draw on are not just economic but are also social, and include their language, prior knowledge, social connections, qualifications, references, information about education opportunities and so on derived from their particular biography (Bourdieu and Passeron, 1977: 259). For some students their habitus and social capital will allow them to feel at home within the routine practices and assumed social capital of university culture, whereas for others the encounter may be alienating. And this experience might vary for any one student depending on the type of university they go to. While all students may experience some element of this alienation in the process of engaging with the new context of academic culture, some students may find this experience even more complex to deal with and potentially disempowering (see for example Erlich, 2004; Tett, 2004; Houston and Lebeau, 2006; Kimura et al., 2006; Moreau and Leathwood, 2006a; Rosado and David, 2006; Antonio and Muñiz, 2007; Bergerson, 2007).

Although higher education has long acted as a gatekeeper to privilege, for example through the Oxbridge system and its close links with public schools and the Civil Service, the opportunities afforded by higher education are being spread to a greater number through the strong tie being made between graduateness and employability. However, the economic function of higher education can also be said to reproduce and extend the middle class, thus maintaining existing material, social and economic processes and relations in society. For example, Tlili and Wright demonstrate how students' motivations to study and choice over institution seem to be associated with their economic and social status. Middle-class students who 'were expected to go to university' did so as a matter of course and chose their university (a traditional well-established one) on the basis of where it was located and the social opportunities it afforded, whilst non-traditional students were motivated by the need to gain employment through their studies and often restricted their choice to their local university – in this case a new university – for financial reasons (Tlili and Wright, 2005: 71; see also Houston and Lebeau, 2006). Those with the money and social capital to do so use higher education as a form of personal and social development, whereas those with limited economic and social resources use it in a more obviously instrumental way to enhance their employment prospects. Such financial constraints affect not only motivation to study but also the capacity in terms of time to do so.

> Our analysis suggests that it is not simply that most students are now undertaking some paid term-time work with the effects of this impacting in a fairly uniform way across the student body, but rather that the extent, meanings and impact of paid work reflect social class differences, with the most negative impacts experienced by working-class students.
>
> (Moreau and Leathwood, 2006a: 25)

The pressure on time created by this need to earn money for essentials whilst studying, is referred to by Bowl (2003) as 'time poverty'.

Bourdieu and Passeron (1977) demonstrate how education as an institution acts as a means of social reproduction, maintaining and consolidating existing power relations in society. They argue that it does this in two ways –

through 'symbolic violence' and 'misrecognition'. 'Symbolic violence' arises where a pedagogic action can be said to be imposed and result in 'inculcation' on the basis of unequal power relations between the educator (both individual and institutional) and the learner (both individual and en masse) and where the 'symbolic effect' of this indirectly serves the interests of the dominant class (Bourdieu and Passeron, 1977: 7). Significantly when what is taught has the characteristic of 'symbolic violence', its curricular legitimacy is seen by Bourdieu and Passeron to be fundamentally arbitrary. Its legitimacy derives from the fact that its reproduction is made possible by existing relations of power and the curriculum itself serves to reproduce these relations of power (Bourdieu and Passeron, 1977: 8–10).

The concept of 'misrecognition' captures the idea that whilst the pedagogic actions of an educational institution serve existing power relations and class interests, this interest remains invisible and therefore seemingly neutral (Bourdieu and Passeron, 1977: 31, 61). Furthermore, this seeming neutrality is shored up by the assertion that such institutions have their own autonomous pedagogic authority. In this way educational autonomy masks its collusion with dominant power interests (Bourdieu and Passeron, 1977: 11–12). For example, when educational discourse and practice use concepts such as 'intelligence' and 'ability' as 'neutral' criteria for explaining a student's success, the effects of habitus and social capital are masked. By psychologising student failure, the institution's role in the depreciation of the student's social capital is ignored (McLaren, 2003: 236). In this way, according to Bourdieu and Passeron, the dominant classes reproduce themselves, and the small numbers of working class who succeed within this system do so because of the hard work they have had to undertake in order to retrain themselves into a new habitus to overcome the disadvantage of prior habitus and social capital that is at odds with the system. The important point from Bourdieu and Passeron is not only that education serves to reproduce class interests, but that it does so in such a way that is 'misrecognised' as neutral, and therefore accepted.

According to Bourdieu and Passeron, certain conditions are necessary for an educational institution to have a role in the reproduction of an arbitrarily legitimated culture which indirectly supports the maintenance of existing power relations in society, whilst at the same time maintaining apparent independence (Bourdieu and Passeron, 1977: 67, 57–67). Some of these conditions are met within higher education in the UK currently. They include:

- **The establishment of a permanent core of specialised agents (teachers, academics) through homogeneous training**   This is happening in higher education in the UK through centralised accreditation by the Higher Education Academy of academic teacher development programmes.
- **The use of standardised and standardising instruments**   Examples currently include benchmark statements for graduate attainment in the different disciplines in the UK and the requirement to produce programme specifications for degrees.

- **The enablement of interchangeability between teachers through the reduction of heterogeneity**   In the early years of a degree programme it is usually possible for most academics within a discipline or department to teach across the curriculum. Significant heterogeneity is however asserted through specialist courses in later years of the degree programme and through postgraduate study.
- **Codification, standardisation and systematisation**   For example in the UK, the Quality Assurance Agency has published Codes of Practice to guide the conduct of teaching and assessment within universities across the sector. In Europe, the Bologna Framework for Qualifications of the European Higher Education Area aims to develop a homogeneous framework for the accreditation of qualifications linked to generic statements of learning outcomes at different levels.
- **Ritualisation and routinisation of educational practices**   Examples in higher education include the lecture and seminar formats, essays, practicals and the traditional use of end of course unseen examinations.
- **The neutralisation and harmonisation of conflicts between ideas through a syncretic and eclectic curriculum which supports the reconciliation of ideas and values through continual dialogue, rather than fully 'realising' these ideas in embodied experience and practice**   Whilst higher education may be criticised for limiting the opportunity for the realisation of ideas in embodied practice, curricula are generally organised according to a logic of argument, critique or inquiry rather than a logic of accretion. It is however the case that content coverage acts as a significant motivation for curriculum development in many disciplines, often in the early years of a degree programme, undermining the possibility of the development of critique and understanding through emphasis on accumulation of facts.
- **The 'self-reproduction' of the institution through inertia, for example through the training of its own teachers such that existing practices are reproduced generation by generation**   We see this in higher education through the role of PhD training in the reproduction of academics and through the ways in which new academics draw on past experience as a student in order to inform future practice as a teacher. The introduction of formal training for new academics itself becomes a normative and thus conservative practice, even though it was initially aimed at challenging this inertia.
- **Symbolic violence and mis-recognition**   Higher education is a space where symbolic violence is both enacted and is resisted and critiqued. Some curricula might serve to maintain and reproduce existing social relations in ways which are against the interests of some of its students, for example through a curriculum which does not take account of feminist critiques of particular forms of disciplinary knowledge. At the same time, it is also a space in which such critiques of society can be fostered and encouraged. Increasing state intervention in the higher educational system through accountability requirements for example challenge the

seeming neutrality of pedagogic authority implicit in the idea of mis-recognition. In this way, they reveal how intertwined higher education and the state really are.

The application of Bourdieu and Passeron's conditions for the implication of education within the maintenance and reproduction of dominant groups in society raises questions about the neutrality of higher education and its role in reproducing a particular 'cultural arbitrary' which reinforces dominant power relations in society. The analysis reveals a tension between higher education's incorporation into the 'skeletal grip of government' (Jamie, 2002) and its related implication as a conservative force in the reproduction of social relations, and between its special role as a space in society in which critique, new ideas and new knowledge are fostered and practised. The interaction in the tension in the institution between transformation and conservation and individual students with their particular circumstances, desires and predispositions creates a dynamic space of opportunity and exclusion, of engagement and alienation for individuals.

The creative potential of this dynamic relationship between student and institution may be undermined by normative categorisations of students into traditional and non-traditional. Such a categorisation suggests a reductive conception of higher education as a structural space providing particular locations for individual students to enter and take up. If the space is familiar, the individual fits snugly into the location rather like the right piece of a jigsaw puzzle. A white middle-class male direct entry student could therefore be expected to fit neatly into this normative structure. However, this kind of analysis – essentially one of best fit – does not take account of the fact that such a student (one who fits the norm), may not in fact experience this space as a natural fit, and their experience may change over time. The 'best fit' analysis assumes a fixity of identity and structure which does not allow for a dynamic and processual interaction between individuals and the institutional context. It reduces social identity to something uniform like class, ethnicity, or gender, rather than maintaining it as something that may be multiply constituted, for example 'black middle-class single parent male with a disability'. Even this more complex identification is problematic however, as it still reduces individuals to types, obscuring the unique and evolving experience of any one individual at any one time. Furthermore, it emphasises the production of privilege and difference as rigid, fixed and determined, thus rendering some as agents of their fate, and others as determined by it.

However, recent accounts of culture suggest that we have to understand culture – and identity – as something that is always in process rather than as something bounded, local and homogeneous (Couldry, 2000: 98–110). Instead, Couldry proposes a view of culture as open, complex and processual, involving flows between people. Couldry develops this view based on Hannerz (1992) who theorises culture as a highly complex material and inter-subjective process, 'culture . . . is the meanings which people create, and which create people, as members of societies' (Hannerz, 1992, in Couldry, 2000: 99). This captures the 'duality' of culture as both 'a set of meaningful forms and human interpretations of them' (Hannerz, 1992, in Couldry, 2000: 99). Culture – or a culture – cannot therefore be seen as unitary, for it is constantly being produced by a dialectic between material forms – for example texts, rules, and symbols – and individual interpretations of and actions through and upon these.

Significantly, however, whilst meanings are 'translated into external forms' and are thus in some ways available to all, these meanings are distributed unequally between people. Culture has been defined as something which is shared, but Hannerz emphasises the opposite. He says of complex modern cultures, that 'Contemporary complex societies . . . systematically build non-sharing into their cultures' (Hannerz, 1992, in Couldry, 2000: 101). This non-sharing is shaped by the differential distribution in society of 'taste, education, income, occupation, and all the divisions in knowledge and status they imply' (Couldry, 2000: 101).

Couldry concludes that:

> We must get away from the idea that the 'primary data' about a culture are a set of '*shared*' meanings, rituals, beliefs, ideas or images, or even the semiotic or semantic structures that may connect them. That is the old model at work, which thinks of culture as a 'place' where certain things are collected together and ordered. But there is no such place . . . Our primary data are not so much particular meanings, which we imagine to be shared, as patterns of flow and the structural forces which shape them.
>
> (Couldry, 2000: 103, my emphasis)

Thus in higher education we cannot assume a shared culture between all members of the institution – whether academic, non-academic or student. Multiple cultures, including multiple disciplinary cultures, will intersect in the academy flowing over, around and with each other in the different interactions that arise between members at different times. However, dominant ways of thinking and their expression, in texts, modes of teaching and study, assessment tasks and criteria and so on, may be differentially distributed between members, so that for some joining this cultural complex may seem natural and fluent, whereas for others it may be like entering an alien environment in which one needs to struggle to live and succeed, in which the activities, organisational forms, meanings, and criteria for success are both opaque and out of one's control.[32]

Sarup's description of the fear of the migrant seems particularly apt here. Others know what they are doing. You do not. Others have a right to be there. You do not feel that you do, 'The nightmare is to be uprooted, to be without papers, stateless, alone, alienated and adrift in a world of organised others' (Sarup, 1996: 11).

If we combine this macro view of the complex processes of social and cultural production and reproduction with an interactionist theory of individual identity formation, we gain a powerful way of thinking about the production of the experience of difference. Jenkins argues that social identity is produced through an interaction between each unique individual, their particular primary and secondary socialisation experiences and their day to day social interactions with other people (Jenkins, 1996, in Anderson, 2001: 136–7). Always involved in the process of identity formation – which is a constantly evolving process – is an interaction between self-definition and the expectations and attributions of others. What is problematic is where individual identifications are asserted but not supported or confirmed by others, particularly where those others are in a dominant and significant position towards the individual (Anderson, 2001: 136):

> Significant in the process whereby people acquire the identities with which they are labelled is the capacity of the *authoritatively applied identities* effectively to constitute or impinge upon individual experiences and internal self-definition.
>
> (Jenkins, 1996, in Anderson, 2001: 136, original emphasis)

The formal and informal social and academic practices of higher education can be seen to 'authoritatively' produce certain identities of what it is to be and act successfully as a student. As individual students interact over time with these constantly enacted practices some will experience their identities as confirmed, some redefined, others as undermined and excluded, and others as crystallised to counter the norm.

This focus on higher education's role in the reproduction of existing social relations in society and the ensuing production of the experience of difference through the naturalisation of a norm of social and academic practice which is differentially available to different members of the university, begs the question of the position of the student *generally* vis à vis the permanent community of the university. For example, does the student experience the university as a welcoming and hospitable place in which they are given help and support to 'settle in'? Or does the student experience the university as unwelcoming and inhospitable, as a place where they feel exploited for their fees, to be tolerated only until such time as they leave? Whilst we might expect the experience of difference to be relevant only for some students, it may be the case that the informal discourse of the institution produces the experience of difference or exclusion amongst all students, through the dualism that is sometimes set up in academics' – and students' – talk between 'them' and 'us', between the temporary members and the permanent members.

The question is to what extent the sense of belonging is possible and actively enabled by the institution. If we conceive of the student as a marker of difference, with some 'more' different than others, does the academy allow for, welcome, constrain or smooth over this 'deviance'? In a review of Peter Ackroyd's *Albion: The Origins of the English Imagination*, Lezard (2004) comments: 'But the political point is this: what matters in this country is not race, but place. Just to be here means to partake in the essence of the islands.

In fact, immigration, the influx of otherness, is crucial to the spiritual upkeep of the nation.'

Such a view of 'immigration' suggests another way of reading the relationship between incoming students and the academy. The 'influx of otherness' represented by matriculation is re-valued as crucial to the spiritual upkeep of the university. This redefinition presents another way of reading the relationship between the individual and the institution. It offers a way of conceptualising social relations and their reproduction in and through the institution, as in a process of flux between permanent and transient members, rather than as purely determinate one way.

I have nevertheless argued in this chapter that higher education cannot be seen as neutral in relation to economic or social privilege. It cannot escape being implicated in social relations and material conditions that support dominant interests in society. And the implication of higher education in dominant socio-economic relations cannot help but produce the experience of difference amongst some students. I end by suggesting that this sense of otherness may well extend to *all* students, especially in the first year.

In this chapter I show how the economic and social functions of higher education operate within the field of power relations in the university context and the consequences of this for the student experience. An emphasis on employability and performance in the context of higher education distorts the communicative conditions of learning through a colonisation of the lifeworld by the system. This distortion includes a shift in student identity from learner to worker, client, and/or consumer of commodified knowledge, and the adoption of strategic approaches to learning that undermine communication and inhibit an imaginative, interpretive and critical stance towards knowledge and society.

The social function of higher education is revealed as complex in its effects. On the one hand the university is clearly implicated in the maintenance and reproduction of social relations in society and in this way, through its own social constitution and practices, privileges some students over others. This privilege reveals itself in the kinds of choices students make concerning the institutions they attend, in the purposes students adopt towards their education, and the experience some students have of difference and struggle. This experience can be exacerbated by an institutional and policy culture which positions and reduces some students to the category of 'non-traditional', and as therefore in some way problematic. On the other hand, higher education provides a special space in society for critique. And a conception of culture and identity as in a dynamic interactive relationship, whilst nevertheless accepting the problematic of what is 'not-shared' within this, opens up further the possibility for creativity and transformation for the individual and society.

In conclusion, I have looked at the complex ways in which the wider social context of higher education, more specifically economic and social relations in society, have their effect on individual student experience within the field of power relations in the institution. In the next chapter, I focus on the institution itself, and its role in the construction of time, space, activity and the self.

6
The institutionalisation of time, space, activity and the self

One could argue that the main purpose of higher education is learning – the generation and dissemination of knowledge through research and scholarship, and the support of individual students' intellectual and personal development. Ideally, the institution should be organised in such a way that constructively and creatively supports these twin purposes. The aim of this chapter is to critically examine the organisation and practice of time, space and activity in the curriculum and to explore the effect such institutionalisation has on the student and the practice of learning. The question addressed is whether the conditions the institution sets up for the activity of studying lead to desired learning.

Examples of institutions include the family, religion, the media, the civil service, and of course education. Although institutions are obviously formed through human action and organisation, they take on a life of their own, and in this way affect human experience and action through the normative practices, conventions and forms of organisation that they come to instantiate. Whilst in early modernity, purposive instrumental rationality held out the possibility of emancipation from tradition, religion, and monarchic forms of social organisation, Weber argued that such rationalisation led 'to the creation of an "iron cage" of bureaucratic rationality from which there is no escape' (Sarup, 1996: 94).

In *Asylums* – a classic work on total institutions – Goffman (1961) investigates the ways in which such institutions (for example prisons, the army, boarding schools) change the behaviour of their inmates. He identified a number of characteristics which in their cumulative effect form the 'iron cage' which shapes the actions and experience of the individual. Although universities are not total institutions, some of the characteristics identified by Goffman as defining total institutions are relevant to our understanding of the ways in which higher education can shape student (and staff) agency, and hence the student experience.[33] The characteristics that are most pertinent to higher education are the following:

- **All aspects of life are conducted under the same authority.** Whilst authority may be dispersed within the university, there is a chain of authority linking the individual student to the university Principal/Vice-Chancellor via their Head of Department, Dean of Faculty, and the Senate. There is a sense in which becoming a student of a university means surrendering some of your agency to its authority and thereby also receiving certain rights and privileges. It also implies entering a position in a hierarchy of social relations – as student rather than lecturer say – and that this positioning will change over time, from first year student to final year honours student for example. There is also therefore a hierarchical relationship between students within the student body, as well as within the academic community more generally.

- **There is a basic distinction between a large managed group, the inmates, and a small supervisory group.** Certainly within universities, students constitute the larger group whose study is managed through the particular curriculum content, timetabling of activities and assessment practices. As described above, there is a surveillance function in operation vis à vis students, and academic staff hold the crucial power of accreditation in their hands. Whilst the degree of formality and distance between the two groups will vary in different contexts, each group is nevertheless still positioned as either in a supervisory role or in a 'managed' role. A further distinction to be made between these groups, and between students as they progress through the curriculum, is the distinction between those who are inexperienced 'acolytes' in the academic practice of the new discipline and those who are the experts. Universities are not however constituted solely by the academic and student community, another important group here are the university managers who may or may not be academics. The presence of this group positions academics as both managed (by this group) and as mediators of management in their relationship with students.

- **High-ranking inmates have more authority than low-ranking supervisors.** Inmates are expected to internalise the norms of staff. To be successful, a student must certainly internalise the academic norms of the discipline. It may also be the case in some instances that a highly successful honours student might be seen to have more authority than a struggling research assistant.

- **Each group tends to conceive of the other in terms of narrow stereotypes.** Staff tend to feel superior and righteous: inmates to feel inferior, blameworthy and guilty. The nature and existence of such stereotyping is likely to vary according to the particular culture of the community the students finds themselves in. However, there is no doubt that academic staff often talk about students as 'other' – in terms of 'they are or do x', usually expressing ways in which students do not fulfil their expectations. As was seen in Chapter 3, students can also see academics as 'other' – speaking another language, being distant, indifferent and so on. Whilst students do not seem to express feelings of guilt, or blameworthiness, many seem to express a fear of appearing stupid and thus inferior. Such feelings may arise from the effects of entering and participating in a hierarchy and culture of expertise in which marks of superiority and inferiority are constantly traded. For example, through grades, selection on to further study, informal assessment – 'she's PhD material', academic funding success, publication success and so on.

- **Social mobility between the two groups is severely restricted: social distance is great and formally prescribed.** Social mobility is possible between the two groups. This is only achieved however through a high standard of academic success and a long process of apprenticeship via Masters, doctoral and post-doctoral study. Whilst social distance between the two groups will vary depending on the culture of the department/ degree programme, at the heart of the relationship will always be the issue of whether one is perceived to be a potential or actual legitimate member of the academic community or not. The student must constantly negotiate an identity on the margins of inclusion.
- **Each phase of activity is carried on in the immediate company of others, all treated alike and required to do the same things together.** Each phase of programmed activity is undertaken in the company of a particular cohort of fellow students in which all are treated alike (for example in lectures) and certainly all are required to do the same or similar things (for example, a particular laboratory task, seminar reading and so on). The general focus, especially in first year, is on the group, with differentiation increasing as the student moves into the later years of the programme.
- **The day's activities are tightly scheduled, with one activity leading to another at a pre-arranged time.** Again all programmed 'teaching and learning' activity is controlled through pre-planned timetabling and pre-booked space. In this way, responsiveness to the desires, needs and wants of individuals and groups is limited.
- **The sequence of activities is imposed by a system of explicit formal rulings and a body of officials whose task is surveillance.** Whilst the timetable of teaching and learning activities is itself explicit, the rules governing this are implicit. That is, what is taken to be the normal way of doing such things is unexamined and naturalised, so that a combination of lectures, tutorials, seminars and laboratory or fieldwork for example are taken to be self-evidently appropriate as a means of teaching a particular subject. Whilst many university academics would deny the surveillance function of their role, many talk about the issue of student attendance and the growing need to enforce some kind of system for monitoring this. Some universities even use a swipe card system for clocking students in and out of the institution and in and out of lectures.
- **The various activities are brought together in a single rational plan designed to fulfil the official aims of the institution.** In Britain at a national level the Quality Assurance Agency and the funding councils require universities to draw up explicit 'rational plans' in the form of

programme specifications for the description of their degree programmes. Whilst these may not express the overall aims of the institution,
they can be seen to represent the articulation of the individual university's
official teaching aims and the plans for how these will be achieved within
different programmes of study.

- **The passage of information about staff plans for inmates is restricted and
  inmates are excluded from decisions about their fate.** Whilst plans are
  published in the form of programme specifications and course hand-
  books, students often have very little control over what is focused on, how
  and when. Whilst students have control over the work they submit for
  assessment, they often have little control over what the focus of that work
  will be, what type of activity it will be, when it has to be undertaken and on
  what criteria it will be judged. Also certain activities, such as examinations,
  limit student control over their own work further by imposing conditions –
  such as time and space limitations – which restrict how a student responds
  to the required task. There is a tension expressed here between the control a student has over their own work and thus over their own fate, and
  the control the institution and the teacher have over the activities
  required, the conditions under which these will be undertaken and the
  criteria and judgements that ensue.

The significance of this analysis of higher education as a 'total' institution is
that it reveals those aspects of total institutions that are characteristics we
would recognise as part of the make up of universities as institutions. This
helps us to identify those aspects of the institutional context that are likely to
form part of the dynamic field of power relations which contribute to ways in
which learning may be enabled or constrained within the institution, and to
how the student experiences their academic life.

Significant aspects seem to be those associated with social relationships,
impersonality, the scheduling and homogenisation of activity, the naturalisation of practices, and limitations on student control.

When the individual enters higher education they enter a position in a
hierarchical set of social relations which distinguishes between academics
and non-academics, between senior staff and junior staff, and between students and academics. The different positions in this hierarchy are associated
with different roles in the institution and are valued differently by different
groups. The student therefore needs to negotiate their identity as student
vis à vis other students and members of staff. Crucial to this identity is the
power of accreditation vested in individual academics and its effect on the
individual student's sense of self.

Institutional control over the learning process and the student's self within
this is also expressed through the timetabling and organisation of learning
activity and the naturalisation of certain practices and constellations of practices as normal ways of studying. Thus when the student enters higher education, they not only take up a certain social position, they also give up a certain
amount of control over their own learning and socialisation process to the

institution and its routinised ways of organising study activity. Thus autonomy and the freedom to exercise control over one's own learning, and its
counterpart – responsibility for oneself and one's own learning – may be
paradoxically curtailed by certain institutional conditions. One way of thinking about this institutional effect on the learning process is to consider these
institutional conditions as themselves part of the curriculum. In other words,
to conceive of these as forming the *hidden curriculum* of higher education.

> School books are tools made of paper. They are vehicles of training:
> they reinforce the school routines of close order drill, public thinking,
> endless surveillance, endless ranking, and endless intimidation. Real
> books educate. School books school. When you take the free will out of
> education, that turns it into schooling. You cannot have it both ways.
>
> (John Taylor Gatto's keynote speech at the US *Options in Learning
> Conference*, 1992, in Meighan and Siraj-Blatchford, 2003: 134)

Books are not inherently alienating however, but once they form part of the
practice of study within the context of the institution, they are positioned as
something that 'must be read' in order to learn successfully. The requirement to read for example transforms learning into work, translating it from
an active to a passive voice. What is significant here is how individual students
respond to these curricular requirements which form the institutionally
structured space-time of study in which learning is to take place.

When students enter higher education, their responses to learning have
already been institutionalised through the experience of schooling, especially
if they were successful pupils. The question is to what extent the higher
education curriculum further intensifies adaptive strategies to schooling, or
enables the individual to be liberated from them and to take control over
their own learning process in a way that redefines the 'obligation' to undertake a particular study activity as an opportunity to learn.

Observational studies of schools, in particular Philip Jackson's seminal *Life
in Classrooms*, demonstrate how the day to day practices of schooling implicitly communicate certain messages about learning and how to behave as a
learner. These studies are significant not only for our understanding of how
higher educational practices *might be doing the same thing*, but also for understanding what this means for what students bring with them from their
experience of so many years in school.

Jackson (1968) describes institutional educational settings as composed
of compulsory timetabled activity, organised in such a way that the same
kinds of activity occur frequently and repetitively, within standardised
environments – for example, that of the teacher's desk and blackboard at the
front, and rows of pupil chairs and desks facing towards the teacher. This
standardised curricular and physical environment sets up limits on the
organisation of space, time and social relations. Limits are also set by rules of
behaviour and certain key controlling roles invested in the person of the
teacher. These roles include those of communication manager – controlling
who can speak when in the class, and therefore also controlling who does not

speak; resources manager – controlling what is available in the class for pupils to draw on; privileges manager – controlling who is rewarded and who punished; and timekeeper. According to Jackson, communication between teachers and pupils is characterised by high levels of redundancy and is ritualised. For example, pupils expect teachers to ask them questions which the teacher already knows the answer to.

Thus while the child is in school, it is as if the child were 'an inmate' who copes by adopting 'adaptive strategies' that then transfer to future life. According to Jackson (1968: 9), 'Classrooms are [therefore] special places' which have three key characteristics, which I would argue are also found in university classroom settings.

First, classrooms are crowded spaces in which the individual participates in learning en masse. There are four consequences of this characteristic. The pupil cannot go at their own speed and has to learn to delay what they need to do, or wait for others. Second, the pupil learns that they cannot do what they want and consequently they learn to deny their desires. Third, the individual's learning process is subject to interruptions; and fourth, it is subject to social distractions. According to Jackson, the strategy adopted under these conditions is to 'disengage feelings from actions'. In other words, the pupil learns to be patient and to control any impulse they might have, to ask a question for example. A tension is therefore set up for the pupil between engaging in impulsive action to satisfy a learning need and apathetic withdrawal, because of the force of social sanctions if their action should break the rules arising from the crowded nature of the classroom. Withdrawal, repression of desire and apathy can thus be seen to be natural and habitual responses to schooled learning and one which the student may well bring to the higher education environment from their own schooling experience. As learning en masse characterises much of higher education, especially in the early years, it is quite likely that these adaptive strategies will continue to be reinforced.

Second, classrooms are places in which one is in a constant condition of being evaluated, both academically and in relation to personal aspects, for example whether one is cooperative or not. It is not just oneself that is being evaluated but so are others. One therefore has to find ways of coping with the evaluation of oneself in relation to how others are being evaluated. The key issue is that these evaluations have an 'official' quality which have implications for one's continuing sense of self and one's future opportunities (Jackson, 1968: 19). According to Jackson, pupils cope by behaving in such a way as to enhance the likelihood of praise; publicising the positive about themselves; and appearing to remain a good student whilst also being a 'good guy' to their peers (Jackson, 1968: 26). Pupils therefore either comply to perceived requirements, or *appear to* comply, for example by disguising the failure to comply by cheating, and staying out of trouble by meeting minimal expectations. Part of surviving in the institutional context requires managing one's self-identity and confidence, and the tension between compliance and peer group membership.

Third, classrooms are places in which the teacher has authority and therefore control over the shape of the daily activities undertaken. This authority is usually wielded impersonally by a stranger and the focus is usually prescriptive, rather than restrictive. It concerns what you are required to do by the teacher and is mostly focused around 'the desk' (Jackson, 1968: 30). Any plans for learning that might be held by a pupil are substituted by the teacher's plans. In this way, work and play become meaningfully established as distinctions in school. The issue faced by the pupil and the student is whether to comply with 'educational authority', or to find an orientation to learning that somehow enables it to escape from its positioning as 'work to be done for another'.

Jackson argues that these classroom characteristics, student experiences and learned strategies constitute the hidden as opposed to the academic curriculum of schooling, and that these two curricula intersect for the learner in the assessment process. In other words, success is not just about learning to be academically good but also about learning to be a 'good student' – on time, helpful, and cooperative (Jackson, 1968: 35). And yet, he argues, the qualities of scholarship are not served well by these coping strategies, for scholarship requires curiosity, poking about, challenging authority, questioning tradition, insisting on explanations, and discipline.

Woods (1990) comes to the same conclusion on the basis of a synthetic review of a range of observational studies undertaken in schools. He describes pupils as having to adopt 'coping strategies' in order to deal with the 'struggle' in school between personal intention and social constraint (Woods, 1990: vii). This struggle is exacerbated where the pupil experiences a dissonance between the dominant culture of the school – essentially middle class – and that of their own social class, race or gender. In a similar study, James (1968) further identifies an emphasis on competition over cooperation, and superiority over equality, as significant values promoted by the hidden curriculum (Meighan and Siraj-Blatchford, 2003: 13). And James describes the quality of the learning experience in schools as unpleasant rather than joyful and one in which incoherence and fragmentation are the norm. Furthermore, in a recent review of hidden curriculum studies in the North American context, McLaren (2003: 212) concludes that the hidden curriculum predisposes children to comply with – or resist and thus fail to have access to the fruits of engaging in – society's dominant ideology and social practices.

Students come to higher education already socialised through schooling into particular approaches to learning and responses to educational institutions. The foregoing account of the hidden curriculum pushes us to consider particular institutional conditions and their potential effects when seeking to understand the student experience of higher education – both in the immediate context of the learning activity, and historically as brought to bear by the individual student's particular educational biography. The question for higher education is whether our own educational practices simply compound these schooled responses or whether we are actually doing something in order to 'de-school' our new students and enable them to enter into a more creative, cooperative, critical and autonomous experience of learning. Margolis et al.'s account of the hidden curriculum in higher education in the United States suggests that this is not happening. They argue that the institution is aimed more at schooling students to accept inequalities in society and their own place within this, than at developing criticality and resistance (2001: 17).

As we have seen so far institutions exert an effect on individuals through the ways in which time, space and activity are organised. In what follows I highlight the issue of *time* as an element in the lifeworld of the student. My purpose is to show how the student's experience of learning is bound up in the particular meanings and structuring of time (and hence of space and activity) at the societal, life historical and institutional levels.

Fragmentation, speed, instant gratification and constant anticipation of future plans and activities seem to characterise the way in which we currently experience the organisation, structuring and use of time in the West. One of the catch phrases recurring in the West over the past thirty years has been 'time is money', implying that unfocused, open, formless time is a price too high to pay when what is valued is efficiency and profitability. This catch phrase emphasises instrumentalism over intrinsic motivation as a driver for the use of time. Deadlines, speed, pressures of work lead to what Benjamin describes as ' "time in hell" which is the province of those who are not allowed to complete anything' (Benjamin, 1973, in Halliwell and Mousley, 2003: 105).

The focus on speed and the related requirement to account for one's time pushes out private time and the space to think and work out opacities of meaning.

> You sense their (critics) impatience at the poem's refusal to explain itself, as if this somehow contravened new rules that all thought must be instantly communicable and language immediately accessible, and therefore disposable: difficulty equals obscurity, and we don't have time for this. But this is the strength and beauty of the well-wrought, challenging poem: it makes you stop and think, it gives you back that private time and space which are so much under threat in our culture.
>
> (Astley, 2003: 26)

Powers (2004) describes our current state as an epidemic of 'real time' which requires every 'second to count', 'every minute to be maximised'. We have even translated this stipulation into 'multi-tasking' and into our technology through the use of split screens, and the fact that we are now expected to be available at any time – through mobile phones or email. Similarly, Lash (1998: 153) describes modern times as an epoch of speed, fed by the dynamics of a constant flow of information which itself appropriates and translates what was once in the field of meaning, for example 'death' and 'presence' into units of information 'alongside other informational units', producing a time of indifference in which 'nothing more is at stake' (Lash, 1998: 154).

Lash argues that the concern with individual subjectivity and the pursuit of a meaningful life in the face of death, which was the zeitgeist formerly in the West, has been replaced in the time of speed by the de-privileging of subjectivity, such that personal meaning has to take its place alongside the non-human, and by the translation of questions of meaning into instances of information (Lash, 1998: 155–7). In other words, 'the atrophy of experience' engendered by the replacement of 'narration by information' and 'of information by sensation' (Benjamin, 1973, in Halliwell and Mousley, 2003: 105).

This transposition of meaning into information, and subjectivity into objectivity may be useful in thinking about the ways in which many individuals now 'choose' to enter higher education. For the individual student, entering higher education is tantamount to a continuing journey through schooling, to university and on to a career or better job prospects. Whilst in a positive sense this enables more people access to improved career and life opportunities, higher education is hereby placed in the domain of life strategy in which it becomes an instrument towards greater economic and employment success. In this way, the idea of education as a good in itself for the enrichment of the person, as a means of enabling the individual to discover and fulfil their potentialities, and significantly as a means to critique, emancipation and social transformation – the ethos of heroic subjectivity – is diminished. Not only are these educational aims diminished in the way they are expressed in the language of the curriculum through the specification of learning outcomes, but it is as if the greater emphasis on employability and the place of higher education in securing the future, has colonised the individual's life course and aspirations to such an extent that following school with university and selecting a degree programme for future career prospects have become naturalised responses to the future. In this way, individuals' lives and life choices enter the field of information rather than the field of meaning. This 'colonisation of the future' (Giddens, 1991) by the inevitability of higher education within the age of speed, deadlines and information essentially produces 'no future', no 'undecidability of the future' (Lash, 1998: 155).

In an interview with Studs Terkel on the theme of hope, Tom Hayden – an American sixties activist – explains the idealism of young people by describing them as 'like eagles, they can see a long way and they don't have any hindsight. They're always discovering something new, and they don't carry as much of the burden of the old.' He then suggests that it is in the next phase of life that we become concerned with money and career and that these concerns of the thirty and forty-somethings 'tempers the idealism of the young' (Terkel, 2003: 70).

As discussed in Chapter 5, I would argue that this idealism is not only tempered but repressed and marginalised by employability's instrumental and material colonisation of the future. This reduction of meaning to information in the life course is not necessarily universal and seems to be implicated in the unequal distribution of wealth and privilege such that the more affluent maintain the privilege of subjectivity in relation to education, whilst the less affluent are constrained to insert their own subjectivities and conceptions of learning into the field of information (Tlili and Wright, 2005).

Once within the institution, the student encounters specific strictures of time, space and activity. University curricula are organised according to particular unexamined conventions, which govern, for example, the length of a degree programme and its organisation into terms or semesters, and the organisation of programmes into modules, or courses, of particular length. Timetabling shapes courses into blocks of lectures, labs and seminars with their own conventional duration and topics are sequenced in particular ways within these. And tasks, including assessment tasks, are timed and sequenced in particular conventional ways too. In this way, the curriculum sets up particular naturalised constellations of prescribed time, space and activity.

Universities can therefore be seen to be operating in what Kristeva (1986) describes as 'linear time', in other words a teleological time which involves the unfolding of sequences of activity towards the fulfilment of particular projects, and what Lash et al. describe as 'intelligible time', the time of Western order (1998: 1). According to Lingis, intelligible time takes its shape according to 'the logic of work'. This is supported by the capacity for memory – which allows for knowledge, and by the capacity for anticipation – which allows for action (1998: 17). Such linear time can be contrasted with others forms of time, for example 'cyclical' time which is the time of repetition and reproduction, and with 'monumental' time which is the time of eternity (Kristeva, 1986). It can also be contrasted with 'biological' time which is the time of the lifespan, of living and dying, and with 'catastrophic' time which is the time of sudden extinction and extraordinary responses to it (Lingis, 1998).

Whilst linear or intelligible time enables the logical structuring of the process of learning into time-bound, spatial and action bundles focusing the student's attention and engagement, and providing potentially necessary structure and progression, these 'bundles' are merely conventional and by their nature contained such that they also potentially limit and inhibit the freer exploration and desire necessary for engaged learning and creativity. There is the risk arising from this of producing a culture of drudgery, work and strategic engagement, especially where pressures on students' time do not just arise from the curriculum but also from many students' need to take on part-time employment and to cope where relevant with family responsibilities (Moss, 2004: 283). The capacity to live creatively requires play, '. . . in playing and only in playing, the child or adult is free to be creative' (Winnicott, 1971: 53). According to Winnicott, the individual gains a sense of their own self in play through the creative processes of interpreting the world and shaping their own action within it. But for play to be creative, it requires open, trustworthy, and purposeless time (Mann, 2001: 12–13).[34] This is also a point made by Meyer and Land (2005: 380) who suggest that the 'teleological' nature of undergraduate programmes does not allow for the more fluid time spaces necessary to students in which to revisit 'back and forth' new knowledge – thus allowing the student to move beyond the stuckness of first encounters through the 'liminal state' engendered by the experience of 'troublesome knowledge'.

Creativity, as described here, is central to the individual's capacity to make sense of themselves and the world around them, to focus on meaning and deeper understanding, rather than on 'getting by' through a superficial strategic approach that focuses only on information. Organised curricular time constrains students at the expense of the opportunity to follow their own learning processes which can determine what is necessary for the individual to focus on at any one time, how they should engage with this focus and within what timeframe. The effect of curricular control over time and space can result in the homogenisation rather than the differentiation of the learning process, with the risk that busy work replaces actual learning and understanding. In this way, learning becomes the new clothes of the Emperor Curriculum. It becomes 'non-learning'.

Furthermore, the logic of intelligible time implicit in university curricula produces subjects amenable to the future strictures of work and who learn to 'manage' their learning within these constraints. This may be seen as the current implicit aim of higher education. The time and space structure of the curriculum can be likened to Foucault's idea of a 'carceral society' in which individual freedom is limited by marshalling space and regulating behaviour (Halliwell and Mousley, 2003: 166). Such a disciplinary technology produces self-disciplining subjects who are able to accommodate to the regime of work – described by Olsen as 'the Time-Master' – but who may have lost the capacity to be 'otherwise' through the exercise of creativity and imagination (1985: 21). As Illich argues, 'school makes alienation preparatory to life, thus depriving education of reality and work of creativity' (1976: 51).

To take reading as an example, Powers asserts that reading is the last place we have within which we can escape the 'virus' of real time, 'We read to escape – if only briefly – the trap of real time, and then to return and recognise – if only briefly – the times we are trapped in. And for an instant, at least, time does not flow but is' (Powers, 2004).

Ideally, then, reading can provide for the student such an experience of 'is-ness', but the problem of course for the student reader is that this escape through reading is effectively colonised by real time, for what is to be read is required to be done within a particular timeframe and towards a particular task, and is implicated in the identity of the self and its evaluation (Mann, 2000). The private space of reading becomes public and thus enters real time. The logic of learning is displaced by the logic of work within the mode of study.

Space and time are also required for the accumulation of cultural capital. Gale (2002) uses Bourdieu's concept of cultural capital in order to examine student experiences in higher education and to highlight the issue of privilege in relation to what students bring with them to the learning situation and how they then engage or not within the academy. He draws on the following definition of cultural capital, 'capital is any resource effective in a given social arena that enables one to appropriate the specific profits arising out of participation and contest in it' (Wacquant, 1998: 221). He argues that the effective transfer or accumulation of cultural capital takes 'extended' time and association with those who have it, especially those who have 'quality' cultural capital. The time needed is dependent on 'time free from economic necessity' (Bourdieu, 1997: 50). Gale's Bourdieuan analysis suggests that this accumulation of cultural capital may be constrained under curricular conditions where there may be little open and free time for contact between students and lecturers.

Not only does lack of open free time undermine learning, understanding, creativity, agency and the development of cultural capacity, it also restricts the opportunity for the development of criticality – the development of the reflexivity necessary for students and lecturers to make sense of their current condition and find ways to be 'otherwise'. In this case, the logic of work displaces the logic of democracy.

> The aim of those working to generalise knowledge as part of a wider liberation both within and outside official systems of learning must therefore be to increase or create critical space and time for negotiation of meaning between teachers and learners and among learners and learners through democratic forms of education at all levels of learning . . . The struggle for the preservation and expansion of critical space and time at all levels of learning is part of the larger struggle for democracy and for freedom of expression, rights of assembly and demonstration, and other human and trades union rights in the new contracting state that is inherently undemocratic, reflecting as it does the direct dominance of private monopoly capital over all areas of social life
>
> (Ainley, 2003: 353).

Ainley goes on to say, 'We are aided in this struggle by the contradiction between the increasingly restricted range of meaning in study to acquire commodified credentials and their irrelevance to the gathering and universally evident social, political, economic and ecological crisis' (2003: 353).

Challenging the assumption that university learning is equivalent to the acquisition of knowledge commodities and credentials, and working with students to develop ways of thinking, being and acting that can productively engage with the crises that face modern society requires a different organisation of time and space within the curriculum. It requires the logic of learning and democracy to replace the current logic of work.

An important element however has been overlooked from these different accounts of the results of the hidden curriculum in schooling and higher education. This is what is learnt emotionally in education by students about themselves and themselves in the world. Holt's seminal study (1964) makes a very strong case for the ways in which schooling produces and builds on the production of fear, shame and guilt in children – fear of not pleasing the teacher through what one does, fear of making mistakes, fear of being wrong. This fear then feeds the development of a resistance to risk and the dulling of curiosity, replacing these with a concern to get good marks, the classroom rewards of a 'gold star' and to be better than other fellow pupils (Holt, 1964: 274). Other factors identified by Holt as contributing to a habitual attitude of dullness include the presentation to children of a disintegrated curriculum of chunks of discrete knowledge, a focus on abstract symbolisation divorced from the child's context of meaning and the repetition of boring tasks, of 'busywork' (Holt, 1964: 275). Holt's main argument is essentially that children are not born dull but are rendered so by the process of schooling, and especially the fear it can engender in the child. As we saw in Chapter 3, the students' accounts of their experience had a similarly rich emotional texture in which the fear of being seen to be stupid played a significant part.

Studies of institutions, classrooms and the hidden curriculum all point to the powerful implicit effect that institutions have on individuals. Broadly, institutionalised activity requires individuals to act in particular ways and under particular conditions which limit their freedom and engender adaptive strategies and psycho-emotional responses which can be said to constitute the hidden curriculum of institutionalised learning. Significant in producing these responses are standardisation, speed, the linear organisation of time and space, learning in large groups, repetition of routine learning tasks, fragmented and abstracted knowledge creating information rather than meaning, ritualised activity and rules of conduct, formal and informal evaluation, competition, and teacher authority.

All students, from any young student coming straight from school to any mature adult returning to formal education after a gap of some years, will bring with them not only the learning they have gained from the formal academic curriculum, but also what they have implicitly learned through the way learning is organised and managed in schools. Whilst different schools will vary in the extent to which their institutional conditions are more or less constraining, it will be the case that most people will come to university with a view of learning that is coloured by this school experience. This is likely to be one which includes the understanding on the part of someone entering a formal educational institution that they will have to learn to cope with and adapt to certain institutional demands that may be counterproductive for their learning process. They may assume that learning is something that is controlled and evaluated by others, and that it involves sitting and listening with others, and keeping things to oneself. And that being successful means working out what is required and either being good at this, or appearing to be so.

Having discussed the wider social and economic context of higher education in Chapter 5, I have looked more specifically in this chapter at the nature of the institution and its organisation of time, space and activities and how these impact on the individual through the hidden curriculum. In the next chapter, I get closer to the activities associated with learning in higher education, and explore the implications a discoursal view has for understanding the student engagement in and experience of these. I then look at the special case of assessment in Chapter 8.

7

Learning as discursive practice

Students learn through language. They listen to lectures; they read books, articles, instructions and notes; they listen and speak, or not, in tutorials and seminars; they write field notes, lab reports, essays and dissertations. They bring to this a particular language biography – how they have used and experienced language at home, at school, with friends, in the media, and they bring particular ways of thinking, making sense of and articulating the world around them. Part of their task at university is to enter a new domain of knowledge and language – that of their chosen discipline and of academic practice generally – and become active participants within it. This involves them in two key processes – interpretation and production. They have to make sense of what they hear and read, and they have to contribute to discussions, and write accounts of their actions, understandings and reflections. In doing this, they negotiate the particular conventions governing these different ways of using language in the academy, at the same time as they engage with new phenomena, new concepts and new theoretical frameworks.

The challenge for the student is how to develop an active voice within these different discourse and knowledge practices – how to become a productive and creative participant within the particular discipline and community of practice they are a student within (Wenger, 1998). In this chapter I examine the demands this essentially discoursal activity makes on students and how these demands can be both productive and restrictive of voice.

Some characteristics of language

We do not stand outside language. We are born into it. Language and society both exist prior to us, and where we are born and to whom we are born will influence, amongst other things, what access we have to social privilege and cultural and linguistic resources. Our use of language will be shaped by our nationality, our locale, our social class, our culture, our gender, our family and friends, our schooling, and the media we have access to – what we read, watch and listen to.

Language is not homogeneous and universal in its forms and rules, and neither is it neutral. How English is spoken or written varies according to whether we are talking about American English, Indian English, or British English; and within any of these countries variation will arise according to region, locale, class and culture. Such variation is not inconsequential. Some varieties of English are valued more highly than others. Within Britain for example 'received pronunciation' (RP) – the accent associated with the educated class from London and the Home Counties – was until recently used as the standard by the BBC. This standard variety of English is also the accepted form of written English. Whilst regional accent is not such an issue nowadays, particular grammatical structures and lexical choices of non-standard varieties of English will not be seen to be appropriate in formal public written and spoken English.

The choices I make in expressing myself through language are governed by grammatical correctness and norms of appropriateness. The blank page in front of me confronts me with a decision – what words to choose and what grammatical structure to follow. Once I begin my sentence, my choice of word is constrained by what can grammatically follow what. For example, if I start with 'a' I cannot follow it with a verb 'were watching' or by a plural noun 'bats'. 'A' has to be followed by a singular noun plus or minus adverbs and adjectives – 'a particularly bald eagle', for example. Certain constraints on our linguistic choices are set up on the horizontal axis by the grammatical relations that obtain within a sentence, utterance or text.

Whilst what follows 'a' has to be a singular noun, there is however potentially infinite variation on the vertical axis in what that noun could be – 'a man/sofa/rat/prickly pear' for example. If 'man' is my referent, more interesting is the choice I might make here – is it 'man', 'chap', 'punk', 'soldier', 'wastrel', 'gentleman', 'hero'? Whilst what I choose will be influenced by my intention as a writer, my topic, my attitude to my subject, how specific I want my description to be, and the linguistic resources I have at my disposal, it will also be influenced by what is appropriate to the particular context of language use – whether I am writing a letter to my aunt, a witness statement or a short story. In this case, choice is governed by social and cultural conventions as to what is appropriate in different situations and to different discourse types.

Whilst all social phenomena cannot be reduced to language, all linguistic phenomena are social. They are governed by social conventions and have social effects (Fairclough, 1989: 23). For example, a statement like 'please sign the register before you leave' is governed by what it is appropriate for a lecturer to say to students and itself has a social effect through its action as a 'softened' order to students to act in a particular way.

Another important characteristic of language is that it is implicit and ambivalent. Except in certain special circumstances, we do not spell things out in language but rely on context, and a shared understanding of social and linguistic norms, and a shared understanding of reality. For example, if you were to overhear the following said by a mother to a child, 'The bath is hot', you would probably infer that the child is about to have a bath, and that the mother is warning the child not to get into the bath. But the mother does not say this explicitly. We can assume that the child understands what the mother says by drawing on their interpretation of the particular context of situation 'bath-time', their prior knowledge of heat and being burnt, their reading of the relationship between themselves and their mother and the expectation that the mother's utterances are likely to be commands, and so on. In other words, being able to participate appropriately and correctly depends on one's reading of the context and on the particular resources one can draw on to do this. Problems obviously arise where contexts, referents, assumptions about reality, and norms are unfamiliar.

We initially enter language within the maternal and familial fold – into the intimate language of home. Later we move into less personal and more formal and public language contexts – out of the home and into school, work, university, public life and the media. In these different contexts we encounter different ways of representing the world – a story versus a lecture or a management report; different ways of interacting with others through language – conversations, interviews, lessons; and different ways of being named, identified and socially positioned – George, Mr Shrub, hey you, students, son, employees. Fairclough argues that these three aspects are 'three main ways in which discourse figures in social practice', producing forms of reality (representation), interaction and social relations (action), and identity (identification) (2003: 27), and all three core functions will be present in any one context of interaction.

Just as I have argued that education is not neutral, neither is language. Language does not transparently reflect external reality, pre-existing social relations and identities, it is productive of these. Language is the key means by which human beings communicate with each other and in so doing construct material and social realities, form social relations and establish identities. Language is therefore central to our sense of ourselves, our capacity to act and interact, and our ways of conceiving of the world. But these aspects may be challenged when the student enters the different discourse domains of their chosen academic subject where their linguistic and other resources may not be adequate, or where they enter a new 'order of discourse' which positions their social relations to others differently. For example a mature adult entering higher education becomes a 'student' in relation to a young adult who is a 'lecturer', and this has social consequences for how they then interact with each other.

So in choosing to study a 'new' subject, an individual enters a new order of discourse, that of higher education and academic practice and that of their chosen discipline. This encounter will challenge their existing representation of the world, their social relations and their sense of identity. Whilst this challenge may potentially undermine the ground the student stands on, if their engagement with it is constructive, it will produce a richer ground, a more differentiated understanding, new ways of acting, and new ways of being. But the negotiation of this new discourse is complex. It requires the negotiation of variation in language, meaningful linguistic choice, conventions of appropriateness, implicitness and ambivalence, and relevant readings of context. And this negotiation will also always entail a negotiation of the student's sense of self.

> Linguistic dispossession is a sufficient motive for violence, for it is close to the dispossession of one's self.
>
> (Hoffman, 1989: 124)

The discoursal challenges facing students are therefore a key place to explore the operation of power within the student experience.

Discourse and power

In order to examine the workings of power within discourse, I draw on the work of Fairclough (1989, 1992, 2003) who has made a significant contribution to our understanding of the role of language in the dialectic between agency and structure. His concern is to illuminate not only how social structure is maintained and reproduced through language, but also how language is productive of agency, resistance, contestation and the construction of alternatives. Fairclough's main contribution is to merge the concerns of linguistics and discourse analysis with those of critical social theory. In doing so, he enriches the textual and analytic focus of linguistics with theory, and the theoretical understanding of social theory with textual analysis.

Fairclough uses the term 'discourse' in two different ways (1992: 5). The first of these is where 'discourse' is used to refer to the particular conventions and ways of representing the world that are associated with different domains, for example the discourse of literary theory or the discourse of nursing. Using discourse in this way allows us to examine the role of different discourses in public domains, how discourses migrate into other discourses, setting up different assumptions about the nature of reality and different conventions about appropriate discourse types. For example, in recent years the discourse of management, associated with ways of talking and writing about human relations and activities within business, is experienced by many as 'colonising' higher education discourses. Universities are now almost universally required to produce 'mission statements' – a practice adopted from business, though it itself having roots in evangelical discourse. Another example is the discourse of employability. This has wrought changes not only in the focus of teaching but also in how what students are expected to learn is described in curriculum documents. In both cases the effects are simultaneously discoursal – changes in how things are spoken or written about – and also social – changes in how things are done and what is taken to be valid within the academy.

The second and more comprehensive way in which Fairclough defines discourse is as constituting – and being constituted by – at any one time, *text*, *discursive practice* and *social practice* (1992: 4). The text is what is produced through writing, speaking or visual representation – for example, the words, sentences and paragraphs you are reading right now, or a conversation you may have had last night. What is seen, read and interpreted on a screen, for example on television, also constitutes text. Discursive practices are what produces the text – the dynamic processes of *production* – speaking and writing, *interpretation*[35] – reading and listening, and *distribution* – selling, posting on the internet, dialogue. Discursive practice governs who or how many authors a text might have, how reference can be made to other texts, under what conditions texts are interpreted, the materiality or otherwise of a text and so on. The social practice dimension refers to the ways in which institutional and organisational contexts influence the production, distribution and interpretation of texts and the ways in which social reality is constructed through discourse. I elaborate on each of these aspects below.

The textual focus draws on critical linguistics which analyses texts to investigate how language can work as a political and ideological process of social control (Fowler et al., 1979). As we have seen already, language is a system of options, such that any selection we make (whether to use the words 'student' versus 'learner' for example) is meaningful, and constrained by social circumstance (Fairclough, 1992: 26). For example, analysing the use of the words 'customer' versus 'passenger' in transport discourse reveals the shift in how railways were represented from that of public service to private enterprise, and a shift in how members of the public were positioned vis à vis the railway. Just as the analysis of the use of the word 'client' or 'customer' to refer to students reveals a shift from student as 'one who studies' to student as one who 'consumes' knowledge, or one who 'pays for the service' of teaching. The analysis of the use of the passive form in 'the man was killed by a bullet' rather than 'Mr Smith killed the man' in media discourse reveals how direct responsibility for an act of violence can be obscured in what appears to be a neutral account of events in a newspaper article. These examples show how language can construct reality in such a way as to appear neutral whilst at the same time obscuring the particular interests served by these different constructions. It is also important to note however that such constructions are also a site for struggle. I clearly remember the first time I was addressed as a 'customer' on a British Rail platform and my rage at this identification!

At the level of discursive practice – how texts are produced, interpreted and distributed – Fairclough argues that this aspect of discourse is socially constrained by the resources individuals can draw on to participate in these practices and by the particular social practice of which the discourse event is a part (1992: 80). For example, when a student writes an essay, they will be constrained in what they can produce by what they themselves bring to this activity and by the particular institutional norms and conventions associated with essay-writing.

Fairclough identifies three aspects of significance to an analysis of power in language at the level of discursive practice – *force, coherence* and *intertextuality* (1992: 78–86). A key function of language is social action. When we speak with someone we are not simply exchanging information, we are almost always also acting in relation to each other. 'Could you pass the salt?' uttered at a dinner table is very likely to be a request, and not a question about someone's capacity, whereas 'Could you do that sum for me?' uttered by a teacher in a classroom is likely to be interpreted as a command rather than a request. *Force* refers to both the intention behind an utterance and to how this is interpreted by the interlocutor. Given that language is highly implicit and ambivalent, in that it can often mean a number of things, a key task for the interpreter is to achieve an *appropriate* interpretation. Fairclough argues that one has to use cues in the situation and one's own prior knowledge in order to do this, and that part of this prior knowledge will draw on assumptions about social structure – who can ask what of whom – and on assumptions about discourse types and what types of discourse tend to follow each other (questions and answers for example). How I respond to different speech acts will thus be influenced by my reading of the power relations between myself and my interlocutor, and what is appropriate to the particular context. How I respond will therefore also either reinforce or challenge these relationships. A teacher might address the following utterance to Des: 'Des, would you like to explain the concept of "ideology" to the class?' If Des reads this as an inquiry, he could say 'no'. If he reads it as an order, he may well acquiesce, however reluctantly. If he wants to challenge the teacher's authority, he could 'mis-read' the command as a request, and reply 'no'. Responding to the force of an utterance within an unequal encounter – where one person is in a more powerful position than another – implicates one in particular power relationships, and involves either reinforcing or contesting these. Being able to read this right requires drawing on appropriate resources and affects one's standing in the teacher's and other participants' eyes. In this way, social relations, identity and representations of social reality are all reproduced through this aspect of discursive practice.

The second aspect highlighted by Fairclough (1992: 84) as significant in discursive practice is *coherence* which refers to the extent to which we can make a text meaningful, despite its lack of explicit markers. We have already encountered an example in the previous section – in order to make sense of the utterance 'The water is hot' we have to draw on our interpretation of the situation and our knowledge of various aspects of reality. This becomes significant in understanding power in language in two different ways. First, if I do not have the necessary resources to draw on to make sense of an implicit statement, I will be disadvantaged over others who do. And second, in order to make sense of a particular statement, I sometimes have to take for granted assumptions about the nature of the world which I do not adhere to. This has the potential to implicate me in a world view which I do not share and in this way enforces the taken-for-granted and dominant position of this view. This could be particularly problematic in a lecture for example where it would be difficult to contest a lecturer's statement, but also difficult in other contexts where there is an unequal power relationship between participants. For example, to make sense, a statement like 'understanding social issues such as poverty requires an objective approach', entails excluding subjective experience as a source of understanding. If one is a student who has experienced, or does experience, poverty amongst a group of students who have not, one is faced with silencing one's own experience or raising one's voice to contest the premise underlying the statement.[36] Both implicate one in relations of power within discourse.

The third aspect of discursive practice identified by Fairclough is *intertextuality* (1992: 84). Intertextuality refers to the idea that texts are made up of bits and pieces of other texts, used either explicitly to serve a particular function in the 'master' text – a quotation for example – or implicitly in that any text always enters into a dialogue with and builds on prior text. Interpreting a text requires one to draw on one's knowledge and understanding of previous texts. Intertextuality also refers to the ways in which texts are transformed over time. The findings of a research paper become incorporated into a student presentation at a seminar, which in turn becomes an essay. Intertextuality, according to Fairclough, is not only a hybridisation of texts, but also a mixing of different conventions governing different discourse types (1992: 85). Entering academic practice entails entering an established tradition of intertextuality, and ways of interpreting and producing such texts appropriately. In a context where originality is a prime value but intertextuality the norm, questions of plagiarism, summary, review, referencing and quotation all figure significantly as challenges for the student. Understanding learning activity as discursive helps us to see where power might operate to limit, exclude, undermine or stretch a student's participation. As Fairclough suggests, power operates at the textual level through the linguistic choices that are made, and at the discursive level through the operation of force, coherence and intertextuality.

Finally, Fairclough draws on the concepts of hegemony and ideology to examine the ways in which discourse is implicated in social practice through the reproduction, restructuring or challenging of what is taken for granted as reality (the physical world, social relations, social identities) (1992: 87, 95). As we have seen in Chapter 4, an ideological understanding of social reality assumes that such reality is not neutral, but is one that serves the interests of dominant groups at the same time as appearing to be natural. Its potency lies in a process of 'naturalisation' which obscures the particular social construction of reality and the operation of interests within this. The combination of the need to seek coherence, to act appropriately in relation to the force of another's contribution, and the implicit quality of language all point to the ways in which language is particularly amenable to the ideological process of naturalisation. The implication of these perspectives for higher education is that what are taken to be natural study activities – such as essays, practicals and seminars – are in fact social practices, evolved over time, that have ideological effects and psychological and social consequences.

Fairclough however critiques ideological accounts of the workings of power because they close down the possibility of struggle and agency by reducing human activity and agency to determination by naturalised ideology. Instead he adopts the Gramscian concept of hegemony, discussed in Chapter 4 (Gramsci: 1971). A hegemonic perspective assumes that ideological domination is necessarily partial, depends on alliances between groups, and on the consent – whether explicitly or ideologically achieved – of dominated groups. Hegemony is therefore subject to the possibility of change, allowing for emancipatory potential, the complexity of intertextuality, and the possibility of discursive practices as a site for struggle.

Within UK higher education, we can see hegemonic struggle happening in a number of areas: the colonisation of academic discourse by managerial discourse; the inclusion of the discourse of employability, personal development planning and citizenship within academic curricula; the requirement to use the discourse of 'learning outcomes' in the new discourse type of the programme specification. Each of these discourses are ideological in their effects. They depend on particular assumptions about the nature of learning, knowledge, good teaching and the purpose of higher education. They have consequences for practice and for social relationships between students and academics, and between academics and the State. And they have consequences for academics' and students' identities and subjectivities. Whilst some of the discourses are beginning to dominate current academic practice in the UK and are thus becoming the norm, they are still contested by individuals and groups within the academy wishing to assert either traditional forms of academic discourse or more radical discourses concerned with social change and sustainability.

The argument here is that much of the student experience of learning is necessarily linguistic and discoursal. I have explored the implications of this by looking at certain general characteristics of language and examining these through a review of the relationship between language and power. I have highlighted the significance of the following for a discursive understanding of the student experience:

- The differential access that individuals have to different varieties of language in society has social consequences.
- Language is based on a system of choices that are meaningful conceptually, socially and individually.
- Language is governed not only by grammatical rules but also by conventions of appropriateness, which will vary according to context. Access to such conventions is differentially distributed and has social consequences for the capacity to participate in different social and discursive contexts.
- Language is implicit. Participation – involving interpretation and production – depends on the reading of its context of use drawing on appropriate members' resources. Differential distribution of such resources has consequences for participation.
- Language has three key functions – the representation of the world

(material and social), social action and the forging of social relations, and the production of identity and subjectivity. Thus any activity involving language – lectures, seminars, practicals for example – involves a student in negotiation of their own identity, of understandings of reality, and of acting appropriately in relation to others, thus forging particular meanings and social relations.

- Language is historical. Entering the world of language, and a new discourse domain, necessarily involves entering existing dialogues and existing textual relations (Bakhtin, 1981). This intertextuality lies at the heart of knowledge production in the academy and is governed by specific conventions. Negotiation of intertextuality is a key task for the student.
- Language is ideological. Sharing the assumptions necessary for a particular text to make sense or for a particular utterance to have the force intended can implicate one in relations of power – in particular world views and social relationships that may appear natural but that may be counterproductive to one's own or to a dominated group's interests.
- Language is a site for struggle. The social construction of reality is, at least, partly produced through discourse, maintaining and reproducing existing reality, at the same time as contesting it.

These characteristics of language reminds us that learning, and the particular form that learning takes as studying in the university, and what this requires of the individual, is a discursive site of struggle.

Learning as discursive practice

Learning is not socially, culturally or power neutral. It takes place in higher education within and through the social and discursive study practices of lectures, seminars, labs, books, articles, essays, reports, dissertations and examinations. In order to participate in these practices, students have to negotiate the textual, discoursal and social aspects of such practices. Interconnected with these aspects are epistemological and methodological ones. Different disciplines will be founded on different assumptions about the nature of knowledge, what can be known and how, and about what count as valid knowledge claims. Such study practices have become naturalised in the sense that they are taken to be the most common-sense way of learning and knowing in higher education. Their conventionality remains invisible.

According to Chouliaraki and Fairclough, the dialectic between agency and structure is partly realised in discourse, for it is in discourse that power relations are constituted, maintained and challenged (1999: 44–5). Given that study is essentially a discursive practice, we can see how the student is always caught up in the agency-structure dialectic, needing to accommodate to and comply with assessment and new ways of thinking and knowing, acting and being, at the same time as appropriating through this a new active voice. I explore this dialectic below in the discoursal activities of listening and reading, speaking and writing using Fairclough's conception of discourse and the three functions of language.

If we assume that any learning activity in an institutional context is always a social and discursive activity, then we can assume that any such activity will involve the student in an encounter with ways of representing the world (knowledge), ways of acting and interacting in the world (action and social relationships), and ways of being in the world (identity and subjectivity). Each of these three aspects may have an explicit content, implicit conventions and underlying assumptions that render these aspects meaningful.

Listening

If we take as an example a lecture on particle physics, the knowledge aspect of the lecture will include explicit focus on relevant facts, concepts or theories; implicit or explicit attention to the methods by which such knowledge can be achieved, including what counts as valid knowledge; and underlying assumptions which make such knowledge, ways of knowing and validity rules meaningful and possible.

The social aspect will be explicitly marked by the fact that the event is a lecture that involves a particular relationship between human beings founded on one being a lecturer with the requirement to lecture and the others being students with the requirement to listen and to note what is being said. It will be implicitly governed by conventions concerning what is appropriate behaviour within physics lectures, and informed by certain assumptions that make this activity meaningful and plausible. For example, the assumption that learning particle physics is best served by listening to an expert in the field give an account of the subject.

The identity aspect is closely bound to the social aspect as the social relations set up by the activity of lecturing cannot help but produce certain social identities for those in the position of lecturer and of student. Nevertheless, the social practice of lecturing tends to produce a certain kind of subjectivity – that of expert for the lecturer and that of passive recipient for the student. In Freirean terms, lecturing positions the lecturer as a narrating subject and the student as an object for the storage and deposit of the narration, potentially closing down the possibility of dialogue and student agency (Freire, 1996: 52). It may also be the case that implicitly, through the content, organisation, and forms of address that the lecturer uses, the lecture as a social event suggests to the students certain ways of being a physicist and a novice physicist which depend on certain assumptions about the discipline, about professionalism, and about academic life, for these identities to make sense.

Thus in order for the student to engage with the explicit material introduced by the lecture, the student has to participate in and agree to certain epistemological, methodological, social and identification assumptions. And they have to do this through a negotiation of text, discursive and social practices. The actual text of the lecture (including visual diagrams and other symbols and forms of representation) will be its structure, cohesion, discoursal signals, tone and pace, and so on. The discursive practices associated with learning by lecture will include making sense through listening, note-taking, copying, summarising, reviewing, keeping silent, and forming and rehearsing questions to ask. The particular social and institutional conventions that govern appropriate behaviour in lectures include keeping quiet, raising a hand to speak, and so on. These norms and their associated assumptions at all three levels produce a naturalised reality that takes for granted the meaningfulness and effectiveness of learning in large groups by listening.

Reading

As with lectures, reading an academic text for the purpose of study requires the student to negotiate explicit content, implicit conventions and taken-for-granted assumptions. The student's interpretation of the text is likely to include negotiation of the meaning of its content on the basis of previous knowledge and experience; negotiation of the social relations and social actions set up by the text between author and reader – whether the author's purpose is to inform, describe, argue, challenge, propose or seduce, and how the student should respond to this; and negotiation of the identities this reading encounter produces for the student – as someone who is subject to the 'truth' of an academic text, or as someone who can contest academic texts and enter into dialogue on equal terms with them. The academic practice of reading involves interpretation of the text itself, the adoption of a repertoire of discursive practices associated with reading for academic study (for example, note-taking, critical analysis, identification of quotations for later use, accurate record keeping, copying, summarising, commenting and rephrasing); and participation in the social practices that frame academic reading – for example to prepare for an examination, to write an essay, to present a seminar paper. What appears at first sight to be a simple private encounter between a reader and a text is a complex discursive and social event having intellectual, social and personal consequences for the reader.[37] For it is usually the case that a student has to do something with what they have read. Just as this is the case with listening to lectures. Thus the interpretive processing of language is necessarily inextricably bound up with the processes of language production – speaking and writing.

Writing

Writing leaves a material and durable trace. Written texts can therefore enter the public realm where they can be circulated, read, analysed, judged and stored. They are often the key means by which students are judged. Student writing has therefore become a major focus of research (see for example Bartholomae, 1985; Ivanič, 1998; Lea and Street, 1998; Lillis, 2001) and student support. Whilst writing tended to be understood as a psychological and cognitive process in previous research (Flower and Hayes, 1981) or as a decontextualised skill that can be isolated, practised and transferred to different contexts, recent approaches to research on student writing conceive of writing as an academic literacy practice. In the case of researchers such as Ivanič, Lea and Street, and Lillis, this perspective builds on the theorisation of discourse outlined in this chapter – that writing is a social and discursive practice, influenced by the interaction between the particular writer and the social and institutional context of their writing situation.[38] Ivanič's work stresses the ways in which the student's identity is bound up with their writing – the point at which the student puts 'pen to paper' is also the point at which they negotiate their identity, how they see themselves as a writer and how this emerges over time as they write and get feedback on their writing. And this can be both inhibiting and enabling. The focus on identity in writing also emphasises the personal and emotive aspects of writing. Writing involves putting oneself on the line, permanently.

Lillis' work highlights the ways in which writing – and especially what she terms essayist literacy practice – is a site for struggle between the student and their aspirations and desires and the regulatory effects of the institution upon these. Just as the implicit nature of the conventions associated with writing in higher education privilege those with previous access to and familiarity with these, and institutionally regulate the access of others, these conventions also set up exclusions as to what is permissible in essayist discourse. In general, "logic is valued over emotion; academic truth . . . over experience; linearity [of argument] over circularity; explicitness . . . over evocation;" closing down of interpretation over opening up of meaning to multiple interpretations; "certainty over uncertainty; formality over informality;" and competition between writers over "cooperation" (Lillis, 2001: 81). Such exclusions shape the style, texture, structure and content of writing, producing texts that are recognisably academic but which, in doing so, potentially suppress the student's desire, emotional engagement with new material, experiential learning as a source of knowing, ambiguity and uncertainty as authentic stances towards new knowledge, and writing as a genuine act of communication with another.[39] Lillis argues that whilst this means that many female students acquiesce to these exclusions and write impersonally (and this may be the case for male students as well), they in fact long for connection through writing (2001: 129).

> Right so I've got to pretend – I think what I should have probably done is to pretend. What you're telling me now, that they haven't read the other bits. And to introduce, 'this is why', cause I've sort of wrote it as if you'd understand why. Like, the reader's read the first part and he knows what's coming in the second part.
>
> (Lillis, 2001: 121)

In this example, the student is realising that they need to comply with essayist literacy conventions which require the author to write as if the reader – who does know – does not actually know. Rather than engaging in a genuine act of communication, they are learning to comply with the requirements of normative academic practice in order to succeed as students and in so doing they learn to repress their authorial voice. In the following example, the student is resisting the same issue, in this case the academic convention of referencing cited authors in an essay, judging the convention inappropriate when what is being written about is already known.

> If it's actual research, something that is intended to be of value – then I think it's very important that things are referenced . . . If it's an undergraduate essay on a subject that's been discussed and looked over for years, then it doesn't really matter.
>
> (Ashworth et al., 1998)

These two quotations remind us that the main purpose of student writing in the academy is not to communicate understanding in order to dialogue with another about the world, but to demonstrate one's understanding and one's capacity to be appropriate within the conventions of academic discourse to another who already knows, but must be addressed as if they do not.

According to Freire, this anti-dialogical approach is anti-human and anti-knowledge:

> Intersubjectivity, or intercommunication, is the primordial characteristic of this cultural and historical world. The gnosiological function cannot be reduced to a simple relationship between a Subject that knows and a knowable object. Without relations of communication between Subjects that know, with reference to a knowable object, the act of knowing would disappear.
>
> (Freire, 1973, in Morrow and Torres, 2002: 35)

From this discussion of studying through listening to lectures, reading and writing, we have seen how even what are seemingly private and individual discoursal activities nevertheless implicate the individual in social relations and in practices which have consequences for them as persons. We have also seen how the 'internal' processes of interpretation are themselves always also bound up with the externalising processes of production, which by being visible, entail the judgement of others. Both of these characteristics are particularly present when it comes to the activity of speaking.

Speaking

Whilst writing puts the author on the line, the author normally has time in which to compose their text and to build their argument, and the translation of text into the material form of print helps to distance the author from the text. Speaking up and speaking out in class puts the speaker on the line under quite different conditions.

Speaking takes place within the real-time flow of discussion and necessitates the claiming of a turn within that flow which will allow enough space in which to make one's contribution. It requires the capacity to judge this right and hold on to the turn. It also requires the confidence and fluency to articulate one's contribution in real time, adapting to the space one has gained. It is all too easy to miss one's turn, fluff one's lines, hesitate and be unable to complete what one was going to say. Alternatively, speaking out might entail entering a great space of silence in which no-one else has dared to speak, one's words entering not a dialogue but becoming an act that may be interpreted as a display to please or support the teacher. In either case, speaking out also requires the capacity to articulate one's thoughts in a way that is appropriate to academic discussion, using vocabulary and concepts that may replace one's vernacular day to day speech, building on what has been said before, positioning one's contribution in relation to that of others, and making a claim to a particular position which one must necessarily be able to defend. Given that the effort to get something said may be all one's resources currently allow, it is likely that one's capacity to respond to questions or challenges will be curtailed. Is it any wonder that some students remain silent within the seminar or tutorial context?

For in this discoursal context, the student's participation is live, visceral and visible, their words – or silence – utterly bound to their embodied selves. Ideally, this forum should allow for slow, hesitant, vernacular explorations of new meanings and understandings. Instead, it usually requires adversarial moves in an academic argument or displays of knowledge to satisfy the questions of teachers, where the power relations between teachers and students are usually unequal, and where differences in gender, class, ethnicity and age may create further complex negotiation of social relations and identification within the student group.

According to Ivanič (2006), it is in this discoursal flow – whether written or spoken – that a constant process of identity construction (or identification) takes place. This happens through the interaction between the identity biography and identity networks the individual brings with them; the social relations the specific context sets up (e.g. lecturer/student; friend/stranger); and the operation of three discoursal processes: how others talk to us (address), for example 'Dr Flower' 'Jane' 'mate'; how we are talked about by others (attribution) 'Jane's excellent presentation'; and the ways in which our talk resembles that of others (affiliation) 'As Dr Flowers has already said, Jane Austen's contribution is to . . .' (said by student), or 'that was a great gig last night, did you go?' (lecturer to students). Identity work, and the preservation and consolidation or enhancement of the self, is a key issue then for any student, and lecturer, in the dynamic of a class.

Breen's (2001) application of Fairclough's model of discourse to the ways in which teachers and students communicate in a language classroom may be helpful here to understanding this social dimension of classroom life and what is at stake for the student. The problem posed for students at the textual level is to judge how and when to contribute in a way that is appropriate to what is required by the teacher. Is a teacher question a genuine question, an instruction or an elicitation? At the discursive level, teachers may exert 'discursive pressure' on students through nomination and the allocation of turns, for example requiring 'overt discursive work' on the part of students. Through this process, students' entry into the discourse is controlled by the teacher, thus positioning the student as passive responder rather than as active interlocutor in the discoursal process (Breen, 2001: 125). At the social level, Breen reminds us that seeing the classroom as a social, as well as a learning, context makes it possible to realise that students are always simultaneously negotiating both learning purposes and the social well-being of themselves and the classroom group.

> They (learners) are therefore obliged to work in order to maximise the learning and social benefits they may gain from the discourse while minimising its potential psychological and social costs. Their selective work therefore reflects their understanding of, and contributions to the emerging culture of the particular classroom group and their own location within it.
>
> (Breen, 2001: 128)

In previous work (Mann, 2003, 2005), I proposed the idea of a 'dynamic of compliance' between teachers and students as a way of understanding how a class can take on a particular style of working which may be counter-productive to learning, for example where students say very little and rely on the teacher to do most of the talking, thus preserving existing social relations and a superficial harmony. This echoes Breen's assertion of a joint conspiracy between teachers and learners, 'creating and maintaining a manageable working harmony through the particular routines and procedures of the surface text of lessons' (Breen, 2001: 128). Breen links this idea to Allwright (1989) who demonstrates how, in classroom interaction, teacher and learners are faced with the discoursal dilemma of avoiding social problems in the group whilst preserving the pedagogic possibilities of learning.

These perspectives suggest that students and teachers are willing to forego the forging of truly constructive learning environments in face to face contexts for the sake of avoiding the potential social and psychological costs that might be incurred by the group or any one individual if the social process of the class were to be opened up for negotiation. Hence the common reliance on the social and discursive norms that govern much classroom interaction. Speaking up and speaking out, whether to contribute normatively to classroom interaction or to challenge existing practices, is a risky and potentially costly business. It puts the individual and their sense of self on the line, and involves them in the complex negotiation of intellectual, textual, social and discursive processes.

In this chapter I have stressed the significance of viewing learning in the university as a social and discursive practice which takes place through the interpretation and production of discourse. I have emphasised how the institutional context affects the student experience through the particular social and discursive practices and conventions required of the student and how these have conceptual, interpersonal and individual consequences for them.

Whilst I have stressed the ways in which power operates through discourse and the social and personal implications of discoursal activity for individuals, I have yet to address the most significant aspect of discoursal practice in the institution. This is the fact that in order to obtain a degree a student has to satisfy certain assessment requirements. These assessment requirements are usually in the form of written assignments, oral presentations, practical activities and examinations. Any work that is not directly assessed, for example reading or listening in lectures, is nevertheless occupied by the fact that the outcomes of these activities are likely to be relevant to and used in directly assessed work (Mann, 2000). Assessment significantly raises the stakes in the discoursal activity of students, bringing the eye of the other to the fore in the social negotiations involved, and potentially increasing the social and psychological costs for the student. It is this special case of assessment that I explore in the next chapter.

8
The special case of assessment

The examination is nothing but the bureaucratic baptism of knowledge, the official recognition of the transubstantiation of profane knowledge into sacred knowledge.

(Marx, in Bourdieu and Passeron, 1977: 141)

... the social cost of assessment ... disillusioned and disheartened losers and calculating, narrowly focussed winners ...

(Broadfoot, 2000: ii)

Indeed, we need urgently to engage with its [assessment] role as a 'social process' that affects intimately and often forever, the quality of an individual's capacity to learn.

(Broadfoot, 2000: iv)

Assessment frames and defines the relationship between teachers and students in formal learning contexts. And assessment and power are inextricably interwoven. Grades, marks and degree classifications translate into self-esteem, confidence and employability; to progression and inclusion, or withdrawal and exclusion. Whilst the university holds the power of judgement and credentialing, in the current ideology of higher education, the successful student can use the assessment system to transform attainment into kudos, recognition, certificates, career and money. A great deal is at stake for the individual – internal psychic health, the future 'capacity to learn', and external social position and economic well-being and reward.

Significantly, as Patricia Broadfoot hints, the power that resides in assessment shapes and distorts the natural learning process, such that learning becomes focused on strategies for satisfying assessment requirements rather than on the object of learning itself. Lave and Wenger see this as setting up a 'contradiction between the use and exchange values of the outcome of learning, which manifests itself in conflicts between learning to know and learning to display knowledge for evaluation' (1994: 112). Through assessment,

learning is potentially separated from the context of knowing and transformed into studying to perform for external reward.

It is therefore through assessment that we most vividly see the interaction
between the individual and the institution and its potentially alienating
effects. I examine this issue through the work of key theorists under the
themes of assessment and social reproduction (Bourdieu and Passeron),
assessment and alienation (Marx), assessment and the production of the
subject (Althusser, Foucault), and assessment and the eye of the other in
hierarchies of expertise (Winnicott, Sartre).

Assessment and social reproduction

According to Bourdieu and Passeron, Durkheim links the coming into
being of the educational system to the moment in medieval times when 'the
validation of results of inculcation' become 'juridically sanctioned' (1977:
56). Thus the conferment of the power to formally assess and validate learning essentially defines the emergence of education as a social institution.
Furthermore, Weber associates the needs of employers in more complex
institutions and bureaucracies to recruit, select and place employees within
hierarchies of specialisms and roles to the development of a hierarchically
ordered examination system which can be seen to offer 'formal equality
for all before identical tests' (1977: 144–5). In this way the needs of a modern
society for social and technical selection can be met at the same time as
the needs of the education system to reproduce itself within 'its own logic'
(1977: 146).

Bourdieu and Passeron argue that such processes can only happen if educational systems can ensure their legitimacy through the assurance of societal acceptance of their examination systems. They do this by 'inculcating'
these values in the social class most disposed to accept their pedagogic
authority, in other words, the middle classes. Willing engagement with the
system will depend on the predisposition of the individual towards education, established through their habitus, and on what rewards are seen to
attach to credentials gained through examination – that is their 'market
value and social position' (1977: 147). The examination is the fulcrum on
which this is balanced.

> In fact the examination is not only the clearest expression of aca-
> demic values and of the educational system's implicit choices: in impos-
> ing as worthy of university sanction a social definition of knowledge and
> the way to show it, it provides one of the most efficacious tools for the
> enterprise of inculcating the dominant culture and the value of that
> culture
>
> (Bourdieu and Passeron, 1977: 142).

Not only is the examination the defining feature of education as a social
institution, and selection and sociocultural reproduction its key functions,

but crucially, examinations, through their arbitration of social selection, are essentially involved in processes of inclusion, exclusion, and social and academic hierarchisation (1977: 152). In this way social selection is concealed under the guise of technical selection, 'legitimating the reproduction of social hierarchies by transmuting them into academic hierarchies' (1977: 153). Bourdieu and Passeron argue that this disguise of social selection as technical selection is most obvious if one examines the 'probabilities of candidature' rather than the 'probabilities of passing' once entered into the system. In other words, the differences between social classes in this respect are most obvious if one examines the numbers of students from each social class at the point of entry to the next level of the educational system rather than at completion. This theorisation of the relationship between social class and education helps us to understand the "likelihood" of any one individual to enter the next phase of the educational system (1977: 156). Bourdieu and Passeron propose the concept of the 'habitus' as the key principle for understanding this relationship and the continuing reproduction of social and academic differences:

> ... the generative unifying principle of conducts and opinions which is also their [academic and social differences] explanatory principle, since at every moment of an educational or intellectual biography it tends to reproduce the system of objective conditions of which it is the product.
>
> (Bourdieu and Passeron, 1977: 161)

In other words, the habitus combines both individual and structural factors. Our structural position, for example our gender, social class and ethnicity, determines our habitus which in turn determines the opportunities we seek and can make use of, which in turn reinforces the habitus. Where someone does extend themselves outside the expectations of their habitus, for example someone entering university from a social context where this is not the norm, according to Bourdieu and Passeron, their habitus will be 'translated' through this experience and the opportunities it offers. However, whilst the individual may change, existing social relations and structures remain essentially unchanged.

Bourdieu and Passeron thus crucially define the education system as an 'agency of selection, elimination, and concealment of elimination' (1977: 154) and the examination as one of the key means for 'translating' social difference into academic difference in such a way that this translation remains hidden.

> Nothing is better designed than the examination to inspire universal recognition of the legitimacy of academic verdicts and of the social hierarchies they legitimate, since it leads the self-eliminated to count themselves among those who fail, while enabling those elected from among a small number of eligible candidates to see in their election the proof of a merit or 'gift' which would have caused them to be preferred to all comers in any circumstances.
>
> (Bourdieu and Passeron, 1977: 162)

Bourdieu and Passeron's theory of reproduction and the role of education and the examination within this challenges the objective neutrality asserted for and assumed of the assessment system, and reveals the operation of power necessarily implied in the institutionalisation of learning. This position echoes the point made by Habermas that the power of dominant class and economic interests within a capitalist society is veiled behind a superficial democracy (see Chapter 5).

If we add to this macro social analysis of assessment, the subjective micro process for an individual of making public the outcomes of their learning for judgement by a significant other, there appears to be a contradiction at the heart of the teaching and learning relationship within the educational institution. Is the teacher there to help the student learn? Or is the teacher there to judge the student and sanction whether they may proceed or not? I explore the consequences of this for the individual and the learning process in the following sections.

Assessment and alienation

Most young children are highly successful informal learners. In the space of three or four years they acquire mobility, oral language, social norms of behaviour, and a certain knowledge of the world around them. They mostly achieve this with no explicit tuition and no formal assessment. They will however seek and receive feedback in the form of repetition, correction, encouragement, discouragement and so on from their mothers and/or other significant carers. Soon after this they enter formal schooling where this implicit learning process continues through the hidden curriculum (see Chapter 6), whilst at the same time they are now formally instructed, required to undertake various tasks by the teacher, and assessed from an early age. As discussed in Chapter 6, children begin to learn certain key things about learning – that it is prescribed by others, that it has to take place at certain times, that it is usually tested, and that it leads to positive or negative marks which signify whether one is good or not. What was a natural, implicit, contextualised and informal process has been transmuted into a task to be done for another according to the others' requirements and is usually associated with judgements of one's self worth. The process of selection and differentiation has begun as has the translation of learning from natural activity to regulated work.

Marx asserts that the individual realises themselves through the process of labour and the creation of a product. Essentially this process enables the implicit self to be externalised and in this way to enter the realm of objectivity (Schact, 1971: 76).

> By becoming an objective fact for himself, this produces his self-realization and individuality.
>
> (Marx, in Schact, 1971: 77)

Whereas a Marxist analysis of alienation would see this individuation process 'perverted' through capital's ownership of labour, we can reframe this in educational terms, and argue that this individuation process is disturbed through the educational system's ownership of the student's labour – through the power vested in it to require that the student undertake certain tasks and the power to confer marks or values on these. In this way, we can see how the formal educational process and its assessment practices essentially alienates the student from their own natural learning process.

Marx makes a distinction between four aspects of alienation: 1) alienation from the product of one's labour, 2) alienation from the process of production, 3) alienation from oneself as a *species-being* and 4) alienation from other human beings (Lukes, 1967). Each of these forms of alienation can be applied to the student experience of assessed work. For many students, study and assessment can be experienced as work that has to be done for others who impose the conditions under which the work must be undertaken, for example what the task is that must be done, when it should be completed, what it should focus on and so on. From this perspective, the student does not therefore own their own learning process but is required to give this up to the institutional requirements within which they are studying. The consequence of this can be a sense of pressure to complete work which thus somehow stands outside oneself, a feeling of not being in control, a sense of doing things because others require it, and through this, becoming alienated from one's self. Given that assessment leads to marks which are differentially socially valued, participating in assessment also risks alienating one from one's fellow students through the hierarchical social relations set up by the outcomes of assessment. By giving up the product of their work to the institution, the student also gives up their labour itself. In learning terms, one could say that thereby the student also potentially gives up or disturbs their own natural learning process. Learning becomes studying, and takes on the quality of 'work' – the logic of instrumental rationality – revealing itself in the adoption of surface or strategic approaches. 'The individual does not "feel at home" in the work he does. He is said to "avoid it like the plague" whenever circumstances allow' (Marx, in Schact, 1971: 90).

As in Marx's theory of alienation, we forget that the assessment tasks required of students – which have become naturalised as common sense – have in fact been produced by the particular relationship between the educational institution and society, the institution's role as legitimator of knowledge, and the exchange value this gives to assessment outcomes. We forget that these have been produced by humans (and can therefore be changed) and that they are implicated in relations of power and domination. The 'use-value' of assessment for learning is undermined by its 'exchange-value' for accreditation and employment (Lave and Wenger, 1991: 112).

'The exchange relation of commodities is characterized precisely by its abstraction from their use-values.' (Marx, 1976: 167) What is meant by this . . . is that commodities are stripped of their use value because in capitalist society buying and selling establishes a momentum of its own, irrespective of the usefulness of things.

(Halliwell and Mousley, 2003: 31)

When students undertake assessment tasks which they perceive to be meaningless and repetitive and whose outcomes are displays of knowledge to be marked, they are rendered objects rather than subjects of their own action.

> Without projects, human action 'is not praxis. . . . And not being of praxis, it is action ignorant both of its own process and its own aim' (Freire, 1970: 6). Such action may be 'adaptive' or 'adjusted' in the biological sense, but such a person is a mere 'object,' not a 'subject' capable of making choices and transforming reality (Freire, 1973: 4).
>
> (Morrow and Torres, 2002: 34)

Assessment and the production of subjectivity – disciplining the self

So far in this chapter I have examined the role of assessment in social reproduction and its potentially alienating effect on the student. Here I return to the theme of learning as discursive practice and explore how this perspective helps us see the ways in which assessment produces the 'subject' of learning.

Assessment in the context of education has certain characteristics. It is something which is required of one by another. In the context of school one has no choice over this, in non-compulsory education one has to fulfil assessment requirements if one wishes to complete a programme of study successfully. Assessment requires one to externalise and make public aspects of one's capabilities. Usually, this externalisation process is in the form of certain practices and governed by certain conditions which are non-negotiable, for example, the essay form and the three-hour time limit of an unseen examination. These forms and conditions are seen to be quite normal and natural. In other words, they have been naturalised in such a way that they seem self-evidently the right and appropriate way to do things. In order to undertake these tasks successfully, the individual needs to comply with, become accustomed to, and as it were absorb these practices in such a way that they become 'normal' ways for them of approaching 'learning'. A further significant feature of assessment is that the purpose of these practices is not only to make an individual 'observable' but to do so in order to judge the individual within a hierarchy of values which will identify the individual as 'this' or 'that', against other individuals. But in doing so, assessment practices produce a certain kind of subject – one who 'disciplines' themselves to 'do learning' in this way, who regulates themselves to 'perform' within a structured 'timetable', who normalises themselves in relation to others.[40] The structure of what is required is internalised as the structure of the self. What is arbitrary has become naturalised. What is demanded, the subject demands of itself.

As we have already seen, ideology can be described as the 'beliefs, meanings and practices' that shape how we think and act and which in doing so serve the interests of a dominant group, or one which is in opposition to it

(Althusser, 1971, in Sarup, 1996: 163). According to Althusser, ideology exists in the material structures of the state, such as education and religion, and through this materiality 'ideology interpolates individuals as subjects' (Sarup, 1996: 163). In other words, ideology is not something separate from social structure or from individuals. It is implicit in institutional ways of doing and thinking and forms the individual through the individual's participation in these institutions across the life course.

Sarup offers the following as an example of this:

> interpolation ... can be imagined along the lines of the most common place everyday police (or other) hailing: 'Hey, you there! ...' The hailed individual will turn round. By this mere one-hundred-and-eighty-degree physical conversion, he becomes a subject. Why? Because he has recognised that the hail was 'really' addressed to him, and that 'it was really him who was hailed' (and not someone else).
>
> (Sarup, 1996: 163)

It is not that we are naturally born into a subjectivity of agency, intention and 'initiative' but rather that our response (or acquiescence) to the call upon us of the institution produces us as a subject of agency who is also subject to this imaginary identity (Sarup, 1996: 54). What seems self-evident is ideological.

From this Althusserian perspective, we can view assessment as a means for the ideological constitution of the self – a self willing to take responsibility for itself and to participate in society on the terms that capitalism requires, in other words unequal distribution of wealth and privilege, social hierarchy, discipline, the linear structuring of time, and so on. At its bleakest we can say that education offers us a fantasy of freedom and greater opportunity, whilst at the same time enslaving us to the requirements of globalisation and capital. The following description of Benjamin's account of the 'phantasmagoric' quality of commodities captures the essence of this perspective.

> ... commodities are phantasmagoric because they conceal the actual, profit-driven conditions of human labour under which they are produced. The profane conditions of the commodity's production are thereby 'transcended', to use a religious term, in the illusory independence of the commodity.
>
> (Halliwell and Mousley, 2003: 107)

Whilst Althusser theorises the production of the subject within a Marxist framework grounded in a view of power as sovereign, Foucault – assuming a circulatory view of power – attempts to understand how the modern subject has been constituted historically through techniques of government and through a nexus of knowledge, power and ethics, or 'regime of truth' (Foucault, 1979). Foucault demonstrates how the shift from concerns with enforcing and legitimating 'princely' sovereignty over territories to the state's government of populations leads to the particular valuing of discipline and the management of population 'in its depths and its details', that reaches down to each individual (1979: 19). Not only was 'discipline ...

never more important or more valorised than at the moment when it became important to manage a population' but also '. . . all the more acute equally the necessity for the development of disciplines' (1979: 19). According to Foucault, knowledge and power are thus inextricably linked. The new disciplines, such as statistics, arise at the same time as the state seeks to manage populations through disciplinary techniques (Ashenden and Owen, 1999: 8). The significant element Foucault adds to this nexus of power/knowledge is ethics – 'action on the actions of oneself' (Ashenden and Owen, 1999: 8). In this way, Foucault suggests that the particular techniques of government which emerge in the 18th century – and which are still current today – enable the state not so much to 'impose laws on men, but rather to dispose of things' (1979: 13) to achieve certain ends with regard to the population, 'without the full awareness of the people' (1979: 18). The forms of subjectivity produced by these techniques are such that the individual internalises this discipline and thus becomes the agent of their own disciplining, acting on the actions of themselves, rendering themselves docile at the same time as more capable, 'let us say that disciplinary coercion establishes in the body the constricting link between an increased aptitude and an increased domination' (Foucault, 1979, in Rabinow, 1991: 182).

Foucault's analysis of the way in which the state orders and disposes people's relation to things proposes two forms of power – individualisation techniques and totalisation procedures (Foucault, 1982, in Rabinow, 1991: 14). Individualisation techniques produce the 'objectification of the subject' in three ways: through dividing practices, scientific classification, and subjectification (Rabinow, 1991: 14).

Dividing practices essentially divide individuals into 'types', thus enabling their inclusion or exclusion from society, either spatially or socially, or both (Rabinow, 1991: 8). For example, the separation of the poor into workhouses in nineteenth-century Britain, or the holding of asylum seekers in detention centres in modern Europe. In the case of education, assessment classifies and thus divides individuals, allowing some to enter the next stage of formal education and others to be excluded. Through this process the subject is rendered object at the same time as social identity is conferred.

Developing in parallel with and informing these practices is the rise of disciplines and the scientific classifications they produce through their theorisation and empirical studies of the human subject (Rabinow, 1991: 9). These classifications take on the quality of 'truth' and obscure their historical production. In education, constructs such as 'Intelligence Quotients' or 'surface' and 'deep' learning approaches would be examples of this.

The third means of objectifying the subject is through 'subjectification', in other words the ways in which 'a human being turns him- or herself into a subject' by an active process of self-formation, usually mediated by an authority figure, for example a confessor, therapist or teacher (Foucault, 1982, in Rabinow, 1991: 11). This 'self-formation' can be undertaken by a variety of 'operations on [people's] own bodies, on their own souls, on their own thoughts, on their own conduct' (Foucault, 1980, in Rabinow, 1991: 11).

Whilst this process is productive in the sense that it can be seen as an active process of self-formation, it can also be seen as subjecting, in the sense that the individual takes on external disciplining practices which implicate them in their own subjection. For example, to be successful in examinations a student does not just need to understand and reinterpret a body of knowledge, they also have to 'train' their bodies to sit still for a prescribed period of time. They have to train their thoughts not to wander in such a context. They have to write using a pen rather than the more usual word-processor.[41] And they will usually comply with the requirement not to break the laws of the examination, in other words not to cheat.

Totalisation procedures bring into being a new regime of power – bio-power (Rabinow, 1991: 17). With the shift from sovereignty over territory to government of populations, the state becomes concerned with the 'fostering of life', resulting in human life becoming something which the state seeks to control and transform through knowledge/power (Rabinow, 1991: 17). This bio-power applies at the level of the human species at one end of the spectrum, and to human bodies at the other. Through bio-power, knowledge and power are brought together in disciplinary technologies which act on the body to produce 'a docile body that may be subjected, used, transformed and improved' (Foucault, 1979, in Rabinow, 1991: 17). Some examples of these technologies include training, standardisation through examination, the organisation of bodies in space, and confession, all of which allow for observation, control and normalisation of the individual. The examination, by making visible the individual, enables their normative classification into a set of hierarchical relations. And the confession, exemplified in higher education by practices such as learning journals and portfolios, brings the individual into a relationship with another who has both required the confession in the first place and who has the capacity within this relationship to pass judgement on the attitudes and activities accounted for.

Regimes of truth associated with disciplinary knowledge (the knowledge that has to be demonstrated in such a way that is 'true') and pedagogic practice (the examination is the appropriate way to demonstrate learning and the assignment of grades is the appropriate way to indicate this) shape the normalisation of the practice of assessment. And the effects of bio-power and the need for the subject to align with an expected norm of behaviour or competence both make the idea of assessment possible, and further reinforce it as an appropriate and 'just' means of measurement. The bio-power exerted through assessment on individuals is veiled behind its naturalisation as a necessary and self-evident practice.

Assessment therefore places the individual in an invidious double bind. On the one hand, as Foucault argues, hierarchical observation and normalising judgement provides the individual with a position in relation to others which 'tells them something about themselves', which gives them substance (Mann, 2001: 15). On the other hand, this positioning also identifies a lack, the place that the individual is not in, and in this way it takes something away. If this experience is associated with failure it may well contribute to a sense of alienation, a feeling of being disassociated from one's work, and from oneself and others (Mann, 2001: 15).

Assessment practices become the means by which students are assigned 'value' and identity within the institution's and the discipline's particular hierarchy of expertise (objectification) and the means by which student subjectivity is produced through required self-disciplining processes (docility). In the last section of this chapter, I explore the profound effect that assessment can have on the individual student's emotional life and sense of self through assessment's implication within the maintenance of hierarchical relationships within the institution.

Hierarchies of expertise, the knowledge function of higher education, and the self

'There is no such thing as a baby.' This startling statement was famously made by Donald Winnicott, a child psychiatrist working within the object relations school of psycho-analysis in the mid twentieth century (Davis and Wallbridge, 1983: 45). What he meant by this was the fact that no baby can exist without a (m)other to care for it. The human being cannot be conceived of in solitude. The human being has to be conceived of within a relationship with another, in this case between the infant and their significant (m)other.

Thus a prime starting point for examining the forging of the subject is in the relationship between infant and mother. A key developmental task facing the infant is the shift from an all-absorbing omnipotent state in which the infant and the world, including any others in that world, are one, to a realisation on the part of the infant of a separation between their self and the world around them and the others that populate it, especially the mother. This transition is necessarily potentially traumatic but, according to Winnicott, if successful, it enables the infant to develop an active and creative approach to its environment and its potential within it. The cost of this going wrong is the adoption of a 'false', compliant self. Assuming that the infant's basic needs for food, warmth, comfort and shelter are met, then the role of the mother or other significant carer is to enable the infant to enter into and participate actively and creatively in social and cultural life. According to Winnicott, this can only happen if the mother is able to provide what he describes as 'good-enough' mothering, in other words, support for the infant's exploration of the world around them which is neither intrusive nor indifferent. Such 'good-enough' support enables the creation of a space between the infant and their environment, a space full of potentiality, which the infant can explore safely and in a way that enables a creative agentic approach to living to emerge.[42]

There are two implications here for higher education. The first is the reminder of the significance (and power) of the 'other' in the being of the individual, in the capacity of the individual to act, in their confidence and resilience, and in their social identity. The second is in how this view of the need to provide 'good-enough' support translates to the formal learning context of higher education. This view implies that the teacher needs to enable the creation of a 'potential space' for their students, a space within which the student can safely and creatively explore the territory of their new discipline. Crucial to this space, however, is unstructured time and 'good-enough' support, support which is enough of a structure to create a space, but which is at the same time unobtrusive enough to do so. This depends on the significant other not 'knowing too much'. In other words, not using their expertise in such a way that undermines the burgeoning and thus delicate expertise of the student. The cost of this is compliance and passivity.

As we have seen one of the limiting conditions often present in higher education is a culture of expertise, expressed in the social relations of the institution, in the credentialing practices of formal assessment, and in the valuing of 'intelligence' and the inevitable production of the culture of the fear of being stupid.

> It's quite frustrating because I wanted to be able to discuss things ... because there were a number of people who, I got the impression, were very intelligent – I was sort of like left out – I just felt that I wasn't equipped to actually put forward any opinions, or put forward any argument. . . . It was quite frustrating and in the frustration you turn off, your concentration goes, which is unfortunate ... and I was just thinking I do not understand what is going on, oh my God, felt so stupid, and I'm not really.
>
> (Mann, 2003: 218)

Within the university, social relations are paradoxically both hierarchical and collegial, expressing different relations of power, most notably between academics and students, and between academics and non-academics. Part of this power is founded on the fact that academics control the examination process, the outcomes of which may significantly influence self-confidence and the future life chances of students. And related to this is the power difference that arises through the lecturer's position as 'expert' and the student's position as 'learner'.

Universities do not just produce 'employees', they also produce, legitimate and reproduce knowledge through research, scholarship, publication, and the accreditation and awarding of degrees. Always at stake therefore is the right to assert something as true (at least provisionally) and the right to contest this assertion on the basis of legitimate epistemological and methodological conventions. This right to assert something as true or to challenge it has to be earned through demonstration of a sophisticated knowledge and understanding of the field of knowledge in question, and the capacity to engage with and contribute to it in a way that is approved of by that knowledge community. Thus the right to participate in the knowledge community of a particular field is seemingly founded on intellectual capacity and expertise. The 'brighter' you are, the greater kudos you have in the institution. 'He's PhD material' is a positive judgement commonly heard in the academy. Intellect, intelligence and expertise are thus highly valued attributes that are differentially rewarded and distributed in the academy through what I term a 'hierarchy of expertise'.

This hierarchy of expertise is explicitly visible in the assignment of titles such as 'professor', 'reader', 'lecturer' and implicitly present through the often tacit and informal judgements made of individual intellectual worth. Everyone in academic life – whether student or academic, or non-academic staff member, is assigned a place in this hierarchy. Thus to be seen to be 'stupid', not 'bright enough', 'only 2:2 material' has to be defended against at all costs. Rather than risk opprobrium by making a careless or stupid statement, many students may withdraw into silence and invisibility. Such an ethos potentially resonates with and thus serves to compound the fear of being stupid, of failing and of making mistakes described by Holt (1964) in the context of schooling – 'dulling' student engagement and risk-taking in the learning process, undermining the very conditions necessary for intellectual development and knowledge production.

If, as Sarup (1996) argues, problem-solving can be seen as an unsettling but active process that is productive of agency, then the existence of a culture of expertise replaces this capacity for problem-solving with a 'network of dependency' (Sarup, 1996: 124). The dilemma for the student is how to negotiate the development of expertise, whilst at the same time assert the right to fail within this process and resist the pressure towards dependence implicit within the hierarchical structuring of knowledge relations.

> The learner is inevitably confronted in formal education with material that is proffered by what amounts to an alien-expert-group and is presented in the terms of the culture of that group. One implication is that in student participation in learning there has to be real surrender of power by the 'experts'.
>
> (Ashworth, 2004: 157)

According to Sartre, human beings are both determination and potential. Whilst human beings have the potential for freedom, it is in the 'look' of the other (which we cannot avoid) that our sense of ourselves as determinate objects among other such objects is produced. The Gaze of the Other sees only the determinate self, not the potential self, 'Of course I still am my possibilities ... But at the same time the Look alienates them from me' (Sartre, 1956: 263).

From a Foucauldian perspective, the eye of the other through assessment can paradoxically give identity at the same time as take it away. It can be both empowering and disabling, but it is nevertheless an effect of power. From a Sartrean perspective, the struggle for the student is to withstand the determinate look of the other of the tutor and its expression in marks, and to exceed this determination through an assertion of the freedom of possibilities to come. The odds against this are high, for assessment draws into itself like a black hole the forces which can so easily undermine the student's developing capacities and confidence. These forces include assessment as the place of social exclusion, where learning becomes work to be done for others, where the self-disciplining of the subject arises, and where social identity and value are ascribed. Assessment is the place where agency and vitality are put on the line.

In Part 3, I draw this critical exploration of study, power and the university to a close by elucidating the institutional forces which seem to foster alienation or enable agency and vitality.

Part 3

Possible futures: concentration or differentiation

Chapter 9 summarises the critical examination of the university as an institutional context for learning by identifying the forces of concentration which tend to *limit* the student's agency and vitality in the learning process and which contribute to an alienated experience. Chapter 10 ends the book by summarising those forces of differentiation which seem to *enable* the student's active engagement in a genuine learning process and proposes five conditions for their realisation.

9

Concentration: the self and the limiting forces of the institution

An ethically and critically grounded humanism is surely necessary, for we have to have some sense of what a human being is to know when he or she is being degraded and what human agency is when it is denied.

(Halliwell and Mousley, 2003: 1–2)

In this chapter, I conclude my critical evaluation of the significance of the institution as a context for learning by arguing that the promise of learning held out by the institution is very often *appropriated*, and in this way undermined, by inherent institutional processes, relations and practices. I summarise some of the key themes addressed in the book as institutional forces of concentration which are alienating in their effects and may limit the agency and vitality of the individual student. I argue for the necessity to view the appropriation of learning and the disablement of agency as an issue of social justice.[43] The challenge for the institution is how to outweigh the forces of limitation with the forces of enablement. I address this issue in the last chapter.

Putting oneself in the position of learner means putting oneself in the position of novice and outsider. The process requires engagement with the discourse, knowledge, and practices of others, most of which will be unfamiliar and therefore likely to be difficult to penetrate. This liminal position is in itself unsettling (Meyer and Land, 2003, 2005). It is bound to create uncertainty, confusion and dissonance, and to threaten self-confidence. Learning by its nature is an emotionally and psychologically complex experience, requiring the combined psychic, emotional, intellectual and physical resilience of the learner. In higher education, this delicate process is placed within the institutional environment, and transforms the 'learner' into the 'student'. Being a student in this environment should ideally benefit the learning process, but as we have seen this is not necessarily the case.

By engaging in learning in an institutional context, the individual now has to negotiate not only the new area of knowledge and competence, but also their new identity as 'student', relations with others, and the institutional practices and requirements which constitute their course of study. Paradoxically, one of the most significant areas the student now has to manage is the tension between learning to understand in order to make new knowledge personally meaningful, and learning in order to successfully complete their course according to the institution's requirements. This represents a contradictory tension between maintaining control over their own learning process and giving this control up in order to comply with the micro and macro time, workload and assessment requirements of their course. The cost of compliance is passivity, boredom and a loss of engagement and desire; but the cost of resistance is the risk of falling behind and failure. Learning is now complicated by study.

The further complication is social. Becoming a 'student' means developing a new identity within the social relations of the institution, social relations which are in the main hierarchically organised according to presumed levels of expertise, within a culture whose purpose is the production and legitimation of knowledge through certain normative practices. The student's sense of self is thus bound to the position in which they are placed by these social relations and by the points they 'score' through marks or appropriate, valued linguistic and intellectual performance. It is no wonder that issues of competence, confidence and the fear of being stupid are present in the studies of the student experience discussed in Chapter 3 and summarised in the Appendix.

The culture of the institution is not just one of expertise. It is also marked by the privileged position it gives to a certain normative 'ideal' student. As one student tellingly said it is not about 'ability' in the usual sense, but 'the "ability" I needed was the ability to take on the values and beliefs of the middle class' (Taking Liberties Collective, 1989: 84). Thus, another complication for a growing number of students is the issue of difference, and how to maintain their sense of identity and engage with learning within potentially alien and excluding cultural practices.

> When those who have the power to name and to socially construct reality choose not to see you or hear you, whether you are dark-skinned, old, disabled, female, or speak with a different accent than theirs, when someone with the authority of a teacher, say, describes the world and you are not in it, there is a moment of psychic disequilibrium, as if you looked into a mirror and saw nothing.
>
> (Adrienne Rich, in Sissel et al., 2001: 18)

Linked to this is the scale of the institution. The student is likely to find themselves one among many thousands of other students in an extended or scattered physical space, where studying mostly takes place in large lecture theatres or libraries, and where often little attention is given to forming social relationships, even within the smaller scale encounters of seminars and tutorials. Loneliness and isolation can be another factor that the student has to deal with, denying them not only necessary human contact but also the rich learning context of peer support and discussion.

Once learning is engaged within the institution, it risks being appropriated by the conditions which surround the activity of study. The learner is confronted with the additional burden of disciplining the self in order to complete required tasks; of managing their identity as a student in order to maintain their self-esteem and confidence; and of working the learning environment in order to make it more amenable to success and/or to their own learning requirements and desires. Learning has become studying and is inescapable and highly present as a task to be negotiated. It is marked out through its positioning as work that must be done.

The echo of the twin potential of higher education to enrich or to diminish runs through all student voices presented in the first part of the book. Consistent throughout them is the significant negative role that assessment, especially examinations, overloaded curricula, unrealistic timeframes and impersonal social and institutional relations have on the student experience. The studies published in the *Experience of Learning* give us an insight into the ways in which the student's psychological context, including learning conceptions, orientations and approaches, inter-relates with the pedagogic context to produce particular learning outcomes. What seems to be added to this psycho-pedagogic account by the student accounts discussed in Chapter 3 are the dynamic emotional texture of the experience of studying and its relationship with student identity, the social dimension of the study experience, the difficulties of dealing with the unfamiliar discourse of the academy and the discipline, and the significance of power and privilege raised by the institutional framing of learning.

One of the arguments of this book is that in order to understand the psychological context of the learner and their experience as a student we have to go beyond a psycho-pedagogic framing of the learning process to include a social framing which highlights the university as an institutional context for learning and the workings of power within this. From this perspective, the student experience is understood as arising through an interaction between the individual and their particular biography, and the particular social, economic, discoursal and pedagogic practices which form the macro and micro contexts of the institution. In 2001, I suggested that the psycho-pedagogic approach to understanding the student experience could be enriched by reframing the concepts of surface/strategic and deep approaches to learning as either alienated or engaged experiences. It seems to me that the appropriation of learning discussed here exactly fits the characteristics of an alienated experience. What seems to be at stake in the alienated learning experience is the loss of the life-engaging desire of Eros to the death-seeking pull of Thanatos. Agency gives way to compliance; curiosity to apathy; creativity and meaning-making to reproduction; in-depth exploration to satisfying requirements; confidence and resilience to anxiety and fear; and participation and contribution, to inhibition and isolation. This is summarised in Table 9.1.

Table 9.1   The dynamic between Eros and Thanatos

Eros	Thanatos
Agency	Compliance
Curiosity	Apathy
Creativity and meaning-making	Reproduction
Depth	Satisfying requirements
Confidence and resilience	Fear and anxiety
Participation and contribution	Inhibition and silence

My concern in this book has essentially been a question of social justice and human rights, the right of the individual in higher education to develop their capabilities in a way which respects their integrity as a human being and which supports the engagement of their creativity, imagination, intellect and passion. Our embodied state places at the foundation of the self the necessity for the fulfilment of certain basic needs such as food, water, shelter and security. Whilst the need for security can be seen to be founded on physical security, this also includes the more intra-psychic conception of the security that arises from a sense of respect, recognition and valuing of one's self by others, and thus by one's self. The self is always implicated in a relationship with another and is reliant on this for a productive and resilient sense of the capacity to negotiate and manage a meaningful encounter with the world and the development of one's life course (Giddens, 1991). The self is born into a particular social and cultural time and place in history, inscribing the individual in ways which will be differentially valued by society, thus privileging some over others as they engage with the world. The historicity of the self is evident in the daily unfolding of the experiences and ups and downs of life, and in the focus on past stories and future plans. The individual comes to the learning context with a past and with hopes for the future. This past history endows the individual with a particular language, culture, identity, ways of seeing the world, attitudes, values and interests which shape and form the personal context which gives significance and meaning to the individual's entry into and engagement with higher education.

> In adult education, where people who had been deprived of any continuing educational opportunity were nevertheless readers, and wanted to discuss what they were reading; and even more specifically among women who, blocked from the process of higher education, educated themselves repeatedly through reading ... both groups wanted to discuss what they'd read, and to discuss it in a context to which they brought their own situation, their own experiences – a demand which was not to be satisfied, it was soon very clear, by what the universities ... were prepared to offer.
>
> (Williams, 1989, in Couldry, 2000: 8)

It is all too easy in the world of academic practice, which holds a common-sense assumption that learning is primarily a cognitive process, to reduce the student to a static and discrete mental entity, primed to the particular current focus of the teacher and the course.

> We're not purely a brain. We're human beings. . . . But they think they can group us in a lump.
>
> (Weil, 1993: 169)

The common notion of the experiencing self, or mind, as an immaterial phantom ultimately independent of the body can only be a mirage: Merleau-Ponty invites us to recognize, at the heart of even our most abstract cogitations, the sensuous and sentient life of the body itself.

> (Abram, 1996: 45)

A focus on mind tends to exclude the embodied and processual being of the individual from the encounter with learning and to ignore the experientially derived vernacular knowledge of the life-world in this. Denying both, what we know and understand from our past experience and that we are sentient and feeling beings, denies the learner's humanity and limits the possibility for learning. Emotion, and in particular the capacity for joy and suffering, texture the daily process of living. Joy may come from success, play, fun, love, friendship, new understanding, a sense of belonging, and beauty. And suffering from lack of recognition, marginalisation, compliance to others' directions, disregard, silencing, isolation, powerlessness, apathy, stress, drudgery, rigid discipline, mistrust, uncertainty as to one's worth, and the constant threat to the valuing of one's intellectual and other capacities – the kinds of experiences expressed by the different student voices in Chapter 3. Important here is not only the embodied, historical and emotional nature of being, but also Kristeva's conception of the self as a subject-in-process, 'subjectivity is an open system, a work in progress, a creative act' (Lechte, 1994: 141–4). Thus, the student's sense of self will be constantly changing within the multiple contexts and interactions of their daily lives, sometimes leading to a restrictive and disempowered sense of agency and sometimes to a potent and dynamic one. Acknowledging the complex and delicate being and becoming of the student requires a valuing of the creation of spaces within which the learner can feel free to learn and which respects their dignity as human beings (Rogers and Freiberg, 1994).

Couldry illuminates the tension I have described between Eros as a life enhancing process of being and becoming, and Thanatos – as a life denying process, in terms of a dialectic between individual self-formation, socially available discourses and practices of self-reflexivity and identification, and wider economic and material conditions (2000: 129–30). He argues that it is important to understand the possibility of selfhood and differential access to its expression by taking account of the interaction between cultural *forces of concentration* and of *differentiation*.

Forces of concentration 'limit the frameworks, the discourses, the images and the practices that are available to individuals in their struggle to function as individuals' and forces of differentiation 'cut across boundaries, multiply options for cultural allegiance, and disrupt the effectiveness of centralized forms of address . . .' Couldry (2000: 129–30).

Table 9.2 summarises the institutional forces of concentration within higher education that seem to limit and undermine the agency of the student in their learning process.

Table 9.2   Institutional forces of concentration

Focus	Institutional forces of concentration	Chapters in which issue is addressed
Purpose of higher education	Instrumental rationality, linking overall purpose of higher education to employment, knowledge production and wealth generation	1, 4, 5 and 8
	Reproduction and maintenance of dominant classes	
Physical space	Crowded and impersonal physical and social environments	5 and 6
Structuring of time and activity	Fixed, standardised and repetitive scheduling of activities and deadlines	6
Underlying logic	Information displaces meaning	6, 7 and 8
	Work displaces learning, play and dialogue	
Social ethics	Attitude of indifference, surveillance and judgement	5, 6 and 8
	'Othering' of student as different	
Social relations	Social distance between students and academics	5, 6 and 8
	Relationships founded on hierarchies of expertise	
	Academics vested with controlling role vis à vis student activity	
Social norm	Naturalises white, middle class perspectives as taken-for-granted	4, 5, 7 and 8
Purpose of communication	To disseminate and demonstrate knowledge	5, 7 and 8
Underlying pedagogic epistemology	Knowledge transmission and reproduction	5, 7 and 8
Social and discursive practices	Academic discourse and practices are assumed to be natural, neutral and transparent	7 and 8

Assessment	Reproductive assessment tasks focus on assessment *of* learning	8
	Disguise of social selection as technical issue	
	Alienation of student from ownership of own work	
	Production of a self-limiting subjectivity	
	Consolidation of hierarchies of expertise	

These forces can be summarised along seven dimensions:

- the purpose higher education is seen to fulfil by society, students and its members and the effects these different purposes may have on the individual student experience
- epistemological assumptions concerning the nature of knowledge and its reproduction, and related assumptions concerning the purpose of communication within the academy, especially communication between students and academic staff
- the organisation of social relations within the academy and its relevance to questions of power, status and knowledge production
- the social ethics governing relationships between members of the institution and in particular between staff and students
- the nature of assessment and its role in the learning process and the pedagogical epistemology underlying the structuring and design of learning tasks and activities
- the affordances offered by the structuring of time and space and activity for reflection, dialogue and inquiry
- the negotiation of issues of privilege and difference within the social and discursive practices of the institution.

Thus the power to diminish – or enable – is exercised within the institution through its purposes, epistemological assumptions and practices, social relations and ethics, assessment practices, the structuring of time, space and activity, and differential access to normalised social and discursive practices.

The effects of these 'forces of concentration' are potentially to disable the vitalising exercise of agency in the pursuit of learning and to produce inhibiting feelings of stupidity, worthlessness, anxiety and the dulling positions of silence, invisibility, pretence, compliance, making do and forgetting. The challenge for the individual is how to overcome these and negotiate the exercise of agency within such potentially alienating conditions and practices. The challenge for the community of the institution is how to transform itself in such a way that the forces of differentiation outweigh the forces of concentration. In the last chapter I address this institutional challenge by proposing five conditions that I argue support the necessary forces of differentiation.

10

Differentiation: the enabling forces of the institution

> Until we know what society is best, we do not know what sort of education is best.
>
> (Dewey, in Garrison and Neiman, 2003: 27)

Whilst it is beyond the scope of this chapter to articulate what form of society is best, this is nevertheless implicit in the proposals which follow. Indeed, one could reverse Dewey's statement to say that expressions of what sort of education might be best suggest a sense of what kind of society might be desirable.

My aim in this chapter is fraught with difficulty. On the one hand I want to articulate what I conclude to be conditions which enable an institutional framing of learning which promotes vitality and agency, energy and enthusiasm, student resilience and confidence, and the realisation of potential. But by doing this I do not want to be prescriptive, nor do I wish to offer a blueprint. The processes involved are highly complex, any blueprint has to be interpreted and enacted, and Maclachlan (2007) reminds us of the difficulties of creating and sustaining such conditions within the existing context and ethos of higher education institutions.

What I hope to do, after summarising the kinds of forces of differentiation suggested by the research into the student experience discussed in Chapter 3 and summarised in the Appendix, is to offer five conditions which might open up spaces for the challenge of limiting forces and the assertion of enabling ones. And this can never be a once and for all project, it is also very much underway in many institutions, and it needs to involve a continuing dialogue towards opening up higher education.

Although my submission is not as desperate as the statement 'I don't know what, but not this', for I am willing to risk a 'what' (Hutton, 1995), my motivation for risking a 'what' is to assert 'not this', not this damaging closing down of vitality at the heart of some students' experiences of higher education.

A culture of learning and inquiry can replace a culture of expertise. In such a culture of learning, making mistakes, taking risks, unpredictability and failure are valued as *necessary* to learning. Lecturers also act as learners, modelling open, cooperative, and relaxed approaches to meaning-making. Dialogue and discussion become central to seeking and clarifying understanding, analysing the significance of material both for itself and for individual students, and for exchanging feedback. Students can be provided with varied opportunities to express and try out their capabilities. Such opportunities include structured, meaningful activities which require cooperative engagement between students who would not normally work together and which provide students with opportunities to investigate and work things out for themselves. Crucially, these activities are given enough time and space for students to feel in control over and responsible for their own learning. Critical recognition is given to the fact that students need support in interpreting and using academic discourse, and that the normative nature of this discourse can exclude and discriminate against certain students. All students are respected first as human beings and are given regular personal tuition which aims to encourage and build confidence. Support is provided for peer discussion and collaboration, and recognition is given to the need to provide opportunities for friendships to develop.

These 'forces of differentiation' (see Table 10.1) can allow students to become actively engaged in a dynamic process of sense-making within dialogical social relations. Learning dissolves as an issue and simply becomes an epiphenomenon arising out of engaged action. What becomes significant is not so much the enhancement of learning in itself, but the enhancement of the student's freedom to learn (Rogers and Freiberg, 1994).

These forces of differentiation can be grouped according to five different themes: purpose, ethics, dialogue, inquiry and resources. I address each of these as enabling conditions for the forces of differentiation in the discussion below.

Conditions to support forces of differentiation

Purpose

Universities are special places in society. Through the principle of academic freedom they have occupied a protected intellectual space in our culture in which individuals and disciplines are free to practise scholarship, inquiry and critique for the purposes of furthering our understanding of the world and ourselves in it, and for the purposes of transforming it. Implicit in this ideal has been an attachment to the 'grand narratives' of truth and justice.

But as we have seen, universities are also implicated within the wider social context through vested interests of an economic, social and intellectual nature. They are given an economic function by government (associated with knowledge and 'manpower' production) and a social function through the reproduction of existing social relations. Whilst academics may claim neutrality for their knowledge work, nevertheless such work is tied to

Table 10.1   Institutional forces of differentiation

Focus		Theme
Purpose of higher education	Communicative and emancipatory rationality linking the purpose of higher education to understanding and transforming the world and the self	Purpose
Social ethics	Attitude of respect, care and support	Ethics
Social relations	Minimal social distance	
	Relationships founded on co-inquiry	
Underlying epistemology	Knowledge construction through inquiry	Inquiry
Curriculum	Responsive inquiry-based process-oriented curriculum allowing for time and space for reflection, dialogue, critique and action	
	Meaningful activities relevant to contexts of practice and student prior knowledge and interests affording opportunities for student exercise of autonomy	
Assessment	Personally meaningful inquiry driven assessment tasks/assessment *for* learning	
Purpose of communication	Dialogue, inquiry and learning	Dialogue
Norms	Acknowledgement that the naturalisation of academic practice as neutral and normal privileges some students over others	
	Action towards ways of differentiating the norm	
Social and discursive practice	Active effort to enable students to penetrate and appropriate academic discourse	
Time and space	Organisation of time and space to provide opportunities for communication with peers and tutors in congenial contexts	Resources

funding processes and to the different ways in which the outcomes of such work can be used within the wider society for good or ill. More recently, as we saw in Chapter 5, the economic and instrumental functions have been in the ascendant, displacing the values of truth and justice. Universities have themselves become alienated.

Whilst I would not wish to naïvely claim that the past was an ideal country, it seems essential to me that we reassert the *process of inquiry* as the founding principle of higher education. Academic practice as inquiry investigates and makes sense of the world and of ourselves in it for the purpose of developing and communicating understanding in order to act in and on the world for the better. Anyone who enters higher education as a student is thus invited to join this inquiry process. The prime purpose of undertaking a degree becomes inquiry into the world through a particular discipline or constellation of disciplines leading to the possibility of continuing this inquiry through action and dialogue in the wider world.

It is clear to all of us that at the present time the world faces some critical challenges. Higher education may help to resolve some of these not by focusing on the generation of employable graduates, but by focusing on the generation of graduates capable of contributing to the huge task of tackling such challenges.[44] Such graduates are confident, vital and resilient; inquiry-driven and capable of critique, analysis and reflection; and capable of informed and effective action in collaboration with others. Higher education's main purpose, as Barnett (1997) has argued convincingly, becomes the enablement of critical being. I would want to suggest that this is best fostered through dialogical inquiry founded in an ethics of care.

An ethics of care

Care has two meanings – care in the sense of 'take seriously and be committed to' and care in the sense of 'look out for and be concerned about the well-being of'. The first meaning is essentially expressed in the strength of the institution's desire and commitment to providing opportunities for its student members to exercise their capacities to learn in the fullest sense of the term. The responsibility for teaching and the support of students would be valued equally with research. The second meaning of 'care' draws on two traditions. The first is based on the idea that since all members of the institution share a common humanity, this requires all members of the institution to 'treat each other well' (Smail, 1987: 143). This is the Kantian categorical imperative to do unto others what one would have done to oneself. It requires a stance of respect and care towards the other, on the assumption that this is what one needs for oneself.

Levinas challenges this categorical imperative and in doing so strengthens the case. He argues against the ontological concern for one's own existence as the basis of ethical relations, for this places self before other, existence before ethics, and knowledge before sociality (Hand, 1989: 4). Instead, he argues for the opposite position, for ethics to be prior to ontology. According to Levinas, the encounter with the other is always an encounter with difference, and thus with the infinite. In this infinite space of difference lies ethics. To do anything other than assert responsibility for the other in the face of the difference of the other, is to eschew ethical responsibility by reducing the other to the same, that is to oneself. It is to reduce sociality to knowledge, and thus to do violence to the other.

> . . . A mode of being and saying where I am endlessly obligated to the Other, a multiplicity in being which refuses totalization and takes form instead as fraternity and discourse, an ethical relation which forever precedes and exceeds the egoism and tyranny of ontology.
>
> (Levinas in Hand, 1989: 1)

Säfström explores the relevance of Levinas for teaching. He argues that 'to be a teacher is often understood as being on the safe side of knowledge' (2003: 22). But acting towards students from this 'safe side of knowledge' is to act in a way that does not recognise the humanity of the student. 'Acting on the safe side' means maintaining 'a non-communicative, non-dialogical, mono-logical act' at the heart of teaching, in which knowledge and rationality characterise teaching, for example by finding out things about students in order to do things to/for them (2003: 22). Säfström contrasts this with a relationship between teachers and learners in which attainment of definitive knowledge is always postponed through the openness of a continuing dialogue which requires risk, listening, responsiveness and answerability.

> Teaching otherwise is an endlessly open exposure, an unfolding of sincerity in welcoming the other in which no slipping away is possible; teaching otherwise is an art when it 'keeps awake' being as a verb.
>
> (Säfström, 2003: 29)

Teaching otherwise requires a stance on the part of teachers and the institution of being open to, and present for, the process of becoming of the student.[45] It places ethics at the heart of the teaching and learning relationship and thus asserts justice as the prime value in higher education over truth and instrumentality (Mann, 2001: 17). This stance reminds us to beware of reducing our purpose in higher education to one of producing a particular kind of individual – 'a critical being' (and thus reducing the other of the student to a type). It reminds us that our purpose is more concerned with openness to becoming and to the support of the student's capabilities in this process through dialogue, action and reflection. An openness to becoming respects the dignity and right to be there of each student; seeks to continually understand each student's particular situation and aspirations without foreclosure; and fosters hope in the individual's continuing capacity to achieve these. Such 'care-fulness' would show itself to each student in opportunities to discuss and shape their engagement with their programme of study, in encounters with members of staff, in the ways in which time and space are organised in the curriculum, in the academic practices they engage in, in the allocation of resources, and in the fabric of the institution.

An ethics of care is founded on respect, welcome and hospitality, openness, listening, empathy, the assertion of hope, and the deferral of absolute knowing through continual inquiry and dialogue. This has implications for the academic's stance to the other of the student, for their practice as academics – especially in this case for their practice as teachers – and for the academic practice of students.

Inquiry-based practice

In recent years, there has been a call to found educational practice on systematic evidence derived from rigorous research (Hirst, 1996). The assertion of ethics as prior to knowledge in the teaching and learning relationship suggests three problems with this evidence-based approach. The first problem concerns the illusion that evidence-based practice creates, that it is possible to obtain definitive knowledge about educational practice and experience. The implicit nature of discourse naturalises the taken-for-granted assumption that robust research can provide evidence for generalisable knowledge statements about education. But this obscures the fact that evidence is always necessarily partial, and requires interpretation, evaluation and embodiment in social interaction.

Related to this last point is the second problem. Evidence-based practice reduces the complexity of practice to a static, acontextual, and universal form of action, rather than as dynamic, contextual, local and emergent in interaction over time. It assumes that practitioners can rationally receive 'lessons' of evidence and apply these in a neutral way. Significantly, since being professional in this way implies being certain and on firm evidential foundations, such a stance disregards the student voice and reduces the student (and the classroom) to an object to be acted upon, rather than an other to enter into a relation with. This stance may also disrupt the openness to becoming, implicit in inquiry, and replace it with the assertion of achievement implicit in a culture of polished expertise.

This displacement of the human is for me the most significant problem. The overwhelming concern with creating a legitimacy for teaching equal to that of research, which lies behind evidence-based practice, essentially reduces teaching from a human matter of relationship and communication to a programmatic, systemic and technological process. It shifts classroom practice from 'How can we work this out together?' to 'What can the research literature tell me to do here?' It suggests a positivist, authoritarian project based on a transmission model of knowledge and learning, supporting the forces of concentration identified in the previous chapter. An alternative is to found practice on a *continuing process* of inquiry and dialogue between teachers and students.[46]

Popper, and others, have argued for a view of the natural learning process as essentially involving an encounter between the expectations of the individual and their experience of the world (Swann, 2003). When the encounter produces 'a problem' – a mismatch between expectation and experience – inquiry is necessarily brought into play in order to resolve this disjunction. The problem rekindles enchantment – in other words motivation and engagement – through the 'spell' cast by the disjunction between imagination and the world. Inquiry produces new expectations – or hypotheses – which themselves then encounter further discomfirmation or confirmation. The interaction between conjectures and the world fuels a continuing process of inquiry. It is this natural process of experimentation and inquiry which can be built on and shaped to the particular requirements and practices of different disciplines. This approach values knowledge construction through a responsive inquiry-based, process-oriented curriculum allowing space for reflection, dialogue, critique and action. The learning process is driven by meaningful tasks – made significant by their relevance to the problems posed by the discipline, the world, and crucially the students' own frameworks of meaning. The purpose of assessment becomes one of supporting the learning process through the generation of feedback to inform the next task, both in its focus and in its process.

In this way, inquiry is both content and process focused. It forms the foundation of the student's engagement with new material and drives the review and refinement of the activities engaged in. It drives student learning and teachers' practice towards supporting this learning. Adopting an inquiry based approach to teaching and learning grounds the legitimation for practice in the community of the classroom, requires attention to and negotiation of multiple perspectives, makes evident or audible the voices of students normally left unheard, and asserts the human over the programmatic. It is necessarily founded on a dialogic relationship between teachers and students, within a culture that explicitly encourages such a dialogue.

Dialogue

> People involved in discussion share knowledge they already have; often this is a series of monologues where each person expresses their views. Those involved in dialogue help each other examine their understandings of the world, develop more complex understandings and, through identifying and clarifying problems and new questions to be asked, thereby create knowledge.
>
> (Barr: 1999: 42)

Benhabib asserts the need in public life for spaces for dialogue or 'moral conversations' providing individuals with the possibility to challenge their existing positions and imagine and enact 'future identities and as yet undiscovered communities' (1992: 8). While she recognises the limitations inherent in this rational project posed by the restrictions on agency produced by social and economic structures, discourse, social relations of inequality and the capacity of individuals to transform these; she argues that what is needed at the heart of this conversation is 'the capacity to reverse perspectives, that is, the willingness to reason from the other's point of view, and the sensitivity to hear their voice' (1992: 8). Her proposal suggests the placing at the heart of dialogue in the academy the necessity for teachers to enter the world of the other of the student, and for students to enter the world of the other of each other, of the teacher and of the subject under study. Such a position combines ethics and epistemology through empathic knowing.

This stance is consonant with the ethics of care outlined above and draws the participants in the dialogue into a relation of co-inquiry in which provisionality, imperfection and the emergent and processual nature of subjectivity and coming to know are valued. Hesitant articulations, risks, stories of experience and unformed ideas become the norm, supporting both expression and the trying out of new ideas in terms of one's own lived experience and life-world. In this way, the dialogic space acts as a bridge between the private and public spheres of knowing, and in doing so enables the development of critical reflexivity both towards oneself and towards one's subject.

Listening is fundamental to this discursive process, creating the very space necessary for the 'summoning of resources' to participate and engage (Barr, 1999). Without listening, the fragile voice enabled by this risks falling back into the 'historical traces of suppressed dialogue', 'closing off the path to unconstrained communication' (Habermas, 1971: 315), what Freire refers to as the 'culture of silence' (Morrow and Torres: 2002: 76).

Ivanič has shown in her work on writing (1998) and in her work on language learning (2006), how identity is crucially bound up with the productive processes of writing and speaking. She concludes that one of the tasks of education is to make possible the holding of different subject positions to those of learner, or student. Speaking from and acting in a different subject position enables the capacity to try out a new identification for oneself, to experience a new form of subjectivity. Creating spaces for dialogic co-inquiry within higher education thus offers students the opportunity to engage in the active agency and critical reflexivity necessary for the subjectivity of inquiry. It enables students to enter into relations of 'transitivity' with their world and others, rather than to be in relations of subjection (Freire, 1973: 17).

One aspect of the world that is not often opened up to dialogue in higher education is the world of academic practice itself, especially the naturalised and implicit norms and conventions governing what is appropriate academic writing, where fluency in these practices reveals the privilege of some and the difference of others. Lillis (2001) proposes the creation of spaces for dialogue to enable 'talk-as-apprenticeship' within which students can contest and query their engagement with new forms of literacy in such a way that might help them work through the 'paradox of literacy' (Gee, 1990, in Lillis, 2001: 158). The paradox that, whilst becoming literate in academic practice allows one to participate, it also implicates one into dominant social practices through the appropriation of learning as study. It entangles the student in the agency-structure dialectic. According to Lillis, dialogue is one space where this dialectic can be disentangled.

A focus on dialogue as a condition for enabling learning assumes the necessity of a social space in which the student is engaged in social relations with others who are also in the process of learning and inquiring.[47] It values the social, embodied and evolving self over the disembodied cognitive self, and asserts dialogue and interaction as the place where the individual can 'move in the gap' between present and future through 'criticism' and 'experiment' and thus address the crucial existentialist questions that any active participation requires – 'who are we and what should we do?' (Arendt, 1993, in Halliwell and Mousley, 2003: 49).

Time and space

Reclaiming higher education as a space for communication through dialogic inquiry founded on an ethics of care requires time and space. It requires the disestablishment of the conventional organisation of time and space into lecture and seminar blocks. It requires a proliferation of congenial spaces for the support of dialogue, negotiation, decision-making and inquiry. And it requires a freeing of the curriculum from the tyranny of time pressure where so much has to be covered by a certain time. If dialogue is valued, then time for dialogue must also be valued. This requires a more open and flexible organisation of time such that planning of activity and time can evolve as the programme itself unfolds. Whilst administrative necessity can be satisfied through the fixing of a time and space shell, this shell needs to be open enough for the dialogic inquiry process to unfold. Creating such spaces allows for R.S. Thomas' concept of the 'recuperation of time' through open and playful activity, displacing the logic of work with the logic of learning and democracy (R.S. Thomas, in Mayne, 2001: 124).

The problem of freedom in higher education

In this book I have asserted the twin potential of higher education to alienate and limit or to enable genuine learning and I have argued critically for the significance of the university as an institutional context in understanding this potential and its impact on student learning and the student experience. Through this focus on the institution, I have highlighted the issue of power within the teaching and learning process. I have suggested that even research within the psycho-pedagogic tradition implicitly identifies issues of power and I have tried to outline through the different aspects of context presented in Chapter 4 how and where power operates. Specifically, I have explored its operation and effects through the economic and social function of the institution; through the special characteristics of educational institutions and the concept of the hidden curriculum; through the institutionalisation of time, space, activity and the self; through the normative social and discursive practices which constitute learning activity in the academy; and through the special case of assessment.

Through this exploration I have identified the limiting forces of *concentration* within the institution and how these may undermine the learning process, rendering learning into study and thus work. I have ended by identifying countering forces of *differentiation*, already at work within different local contexts within institutions, and suggested five enabling conditions for opening higher education up towards the support of agency, potentiality and vitality. These are the realignment of the purpose of higher education towards a communicative and emancipatory rationality; the adoption of an ethics of care as a foundation for practice; the placing of inquiry and dialogue at the heart of teaching and learning; and the reallocation of the material resources of time and space to support this dialogic inquiry process.

At the heart of this account have been three concerns. First, I have sought to place questions of teaching and learning within the discourse of ethics and justice, arguing that any diminishment of the student produced by the institution should be understood as a question of human rights in which the freedom of the individual may be compromised. This focus on the integrity of the human within the educational process reminds us that teaching and learning are social processes that take place through relations between human beings, but that these are however situated within a particular social and institutional context which acts upon this relationship.

The second concern has been to emphasise the necessity of taking account of the institution as the context for learning in any research which seeks to understand the experience of learning in higher education, or the student's experience more generally. Neglecting this dimension reduces understanding and explanation of these phenomena to student characteristics, pedagogic practices, or to relations between the two. It avoids the complexity of the teaching and learning process – its social, historical and human dimensions, and the workings of power within these. In doing so, such avoidance makes it harder to understand why things seem to go wrong for many students. It neglects the issue of justice and compounds the view of institutionalised education as neutral.

My third concern has been to show how complex the teaching and learning process is and therefore how significant it is to try to understand any problem in practice – for example silence in seminars, student non-attendance, plagiarism and so on – as issues that arise through the interrelationship between individuals and the particular conventions and practices of the institution. It requires understanding such issues as the product of an agency-structure dialectic. As neither the product of individual malfeisance, or the product of institutional practice alone, but as the product of a dynamic relationship between the two, grounded in the complexity of the pushes and pulls of the wider social, economic, and political context. Inquiring into such issues by combining the understanding that can be gained from listening to the voices of the different parties involved with an analysis of the forces explored in this book, might provide a rich understanding that can lead to any necessary changes in culture, conventions, relations and practices in the institution. It is these that I have tried to identify through the forces of differentiation and the enabling conditions discussed in this final chapter.

There is of course a paradox here. Whilst the analysis in this book suggests the need to foster enabling conditions to counter limiting forces of concentration in the institution, it is those very forces which mitigate against these, and help us understand why this is so very hard to do. Furthermore, whilst we seek to engender freedom, agency and responsibility in our students, this purpose is in itself a choice we have made on behalf of them. Inevitably, as individuals within education, we are caught up in the dialectic between agency and structure. Our day to day actions are constrained by the weight of history, and social and economic relations and structures. And yet, we are also able to challenge these through the exercise of our agency in inquiry and dialogue. As Foucault reminds us, liberty is not something that can be bestowed it is 'what must be exercised' (Foucault, 1999: 135).

To assume we can easily undo the problem of power in education is naïve, and to propose a categorical solution blinds us to alternatives that are as yet unformed. This is a further justification for the necessity of dialogue, inquiry and care within the learning and teaching relationship. For it is through these processes that students and teachers can together forge their presents and their futures, and find ways to be otherwise.

Notes

1 This is an extract from a learning journal kept by a first-year arts student. See Chapter 3 and the Appendix for more information on this.
2 I use 'higher education' to refer to university level education.
3 A levels are the examinations taken at the end of secondary schooling in the English education system.
4 See for example Holt, 1964; Snyder, 1966; Jackson, 1968; Freire, 1970; Lacey, 1970; Young, 1971; Bernstein, 1975; Bowles and Gintis, 1976; Illich, 1976; Bourdieu and Passeron, 1977; Willis, 1977; Sarup, 1978; Apple, 1979; McLaren, 1980; Giroux, 1983, amongst others.
5 Lea (2005) also makes this point.
6 My thanks to my colleague Jane Pritchard for reminding me of this.
7 Using different terminology, Weil (1993: 164–5) describes this alienating or engaging experience in education as either one of 'disjunction' or of 'integration' brought about by 'miseducation' or 'education'.
8 See for example, Baudrillard, 1987, in Halliwell and Mousley, 2003: 6–7.
9 Briefly, forces of concentration are forces in society which limit agency and freedom, and forces of differentiation are those which support such agency (Couldry, 2000: 129–30). See Chapter 9 for a discussion of these concepts.
10 I owe this perspective to Stuart Hall who writes, 'The object of [my] work is . . . not to generate another good theory, but to give a better theorized account of concrete historical reality' (Hall, 1988, in Halliwell and Mousley, 2003: 91–2).
11 This is the second edition of this book. The first edition was published in 1984. The research presented in the book was either first published in this first edition or earlier in various journals. In all cases, in this chapter the relevant research is referred to as in the 1997 edition.
12 This research was originally reported in 1976 (Marton and Saljo, 1976).
13 Also relevant here are Anderson's (1997) findings that the perceived quality of the student's relationship with tutors is significant, and Hodgson's (1997) that the extent to which students perceive lecturers as able to create an experience of vicarious relevance is important for engaging students in lectures.
14 This data was collected for the purpose of aiding academic staff with the evaluation of their teaching. The data has not been systematically analysed as part of a wider research study. The quotations presented were identified – in the same

way as those from published studies – as offering an insight into the student experience. All quotes from this data are identifiable by the lack of published reference. Further information on this data is available at the end of the Table of Studies of the Student Experience in the Appendix.

15 For each quotation, I include reference to the original research and any relevant contextualising information.

16 This term is borrowed from Gale (2002: 69).

17 Cousin (2006) uses this term from Hall (1992) to make the point that it is no longer possible to think of identity as 'static and pure', instead it is more appropriate to think of identity as being culturally hybrid.

18 A recent literature review of the first-year experience emphasises student preference for active learning in the context of teamwork and projects (Harvey et al., 2006: 8).

19 As we have already seen, Prosser and Trigwell (1999) make the distinction between external context and the subjective experience of context by referring to the particular perception a student has of their context as the student's *situation.*

20 Chapter 7 offers a detailed discussion of the nature of language, discourse and discursive practice and its relevance to understanding the student experience.

21 Adapted from Fairclough, 1989, 1992 and Lillis, 2001.

22 I define agency as the capacity of human beings to act autonomously, free from control, and through their actions to transform their world. I define social structure as existing determinate social and economic relations, and the social and discursive practices and conventions, the ideologies, and the discourses which serve to maintain these. See the section on power in this chapter for a discussion of ideology and Chapter 7 for a discussion of social and discursive practices and discourse.

23 See for example Fairclough, 1989, 1992, 1995 and Chouliaraki and Fairclough, 1999 for such an account of the relationship between structure and agency.

24 This inclusion of the issue of power is a taken-for-granted in critical social theory and critical discourse analysis, see for example Fairclough 1989 and 1992. Barton and Tusting (2005) have addressed this issue with regard to the communities of practice literature from a discourse and literacy perspective.

25 UNESCO (2006) indicates that there is a general trend internationally towards an increase in the numbers of students in higher education.

26 The shift towards employability, marketisation, entrepreneurialism and managerialism in higher education is also evident in Europe (Miclea, 2004) and Australia (Duke, 2004).

27 See also Rassmussen, 1990, Chapters 2 and 3, and Habermas, 1984 and 1987.

28 See McLean (2006) for a detailed critique of contemporary higher education from a Habermasian point of view.

29 Taylor et al. (2002) and Evans (2004) also offer critiques focused on the effects of bureaucratisation, managerialism and the dominance of economic values on contemporary higher education.

30 According to the UK Higher Education Statistics Agency (HESA) (2008), figures for 2006/07 indicate that female professors are 17.5% of the total academic population, and female senior lecturers 36.8%. The majority of part-time staff are still women (41.8% of female academics versus 26.8% of male academics); and HESA (2007) reports that ethnic minority academic staff represent 10.70% of the total academic staff population in 2005/06.

31 For example, working-class students, students whose parents did not themselves

go to university, non-white students, students with a disability and mature students.

32 See Leathwood and O'Connell (2003) for an account of the 'non-traditional' student experience as one of *struggle* against financial difficulties, lack of confidence, lack of support and a general institutional culture that sees 'new' students as problematic.

33 See Meighan and Siraj-Blatchford, 2003: 128–9 for a summary of these.

34 Case and Gunstone report a mini teaching experiment in which students were given unlimited time in which to undertake a test. This experience was positively valued by the students and enabled them to come to an appreciation of what they really understood about the subject in question (2003: 66–7).

35 Fairclough uses the term 'consumption', I prefer to use the term 'interpretation' with its more active connotation.

36 Adapted from Taking Liberties Collective (1989: 100).

37 See Mann (2000) for a discussion of the impact of assessment on reading, and Haggis (2006: 529) for a discussion of the alienation associated with reading academic texts for some students.

38 See Lea (2005: 191–4) for a recent review of this work.

39 In a study of undergraduate essay writing, Read et al. (2001) conclude that many students withhold the expression of their views in writing for fear that they will be penalised by staff who do not share their views. They learn to write from the tutor's voice rather than their own.

40 This description draws on Foucault's theorisation of disciplinary practices and the self-disciplining subject, as discussed in Chapter 4.

41 My thanks to Dai Hounsell and Simon van Heyningen for this observation.

42 See Davis and Wallbridge (1983) for an account of Winnicott's theory of child development and Winnicott (1971) for the relationship between play and the development of the social and cultural self.

43 McLean (2006) and Walker (2006) both emphasise the need to view the student experience of higher education as an issue of social justice.

44 Taylor et al. (2002: 161) argue for the purpose of higher education to be one of radical social purpose with the aim of enabling students to lead fulfilling lives at the same time as being able to reflexively critique and identify what is their own best interests, those of their community and society, whilst Delanty (2001) discusses the purpose of universities as fostering citizenship and the capacity for reflexivity at a societal level through scientific and cultural processes.

45 Barnett (2005: 795) offers a related argument by proposing the assertion of ontology over epistemology in the pedagogic relationship, in other words for teachers to value and affirm students as human beings over a reduction of students to just knowers.

46 Collective inquiry and dialogue is also advocated by Haggis (2006).

47 The full participation of the student in the scholarly community of research and inquiry is proposed by Brew (2006) as a way of integrating the relationship between research and teaching.

Appendix

Studies of the student experience (SE) in higher education referred to in Chapter 3 and elsewhere

Researchers	Year	Focus	Method[1]	Subjects	Number	Gender[2]	Location[3]	Race/Ethnicity/Nationality	Class	Age	Level
Bergerson	2007	Working class SE of college	Instrumental case study Semi-structured interviews Student journals Observation		1	F	USA	Hispanic	Low socio-economic Rural		UG
Case	2007	SE of learning	Semi-structured interviews	Chemical engineering	36		South Africa	Black African Coloured Indian White			3rd year UG
Gill	2007	SE of intercultural learning	Participant observation In-depth interviews		10		UK	Chinese			PG
Goode	2007	Students with disabilities early experiences	Interviews Video-recording		20	14 F 6 M	UK				UGs 1 PG 1 Graduate
Greasley & Ashworth	2007	SE of lifeworld	Three in-depth interviews	Business studies	6		UK				UG

Hsieh	2007	SE of invisibility and struggle of overseas student	Case study	Dietetics	1	F	USA	Chinese			Internship/ Graduate studies
Johnson	2007	Women of colour SE of science classes	Interviews and non-participant observation	Science enrichment programme for high achieving students	16	F	USA	Black Latina American Indian			UG
Kitto & Saltmarsh	2007	SE of online examination	Interviews	Technical subjects	2	M	Australia			19–20 yrs	UG
Lee & Rice	2007	SE of discrimination	Case study of research university (Survey) Interviews	International students	Survey (501) Interviews (24)	14 F 10 M	USA	India East Asia Latin America Europe Africa Gulf Region Caribbean Canada New Zealand			UG and PG
Mayuzumi et al.	2007	SE of difference of Japanese students	Autoethnography through dialogue	Education	4	F	Canada	Japanese			
Solomon	2007	SE of identity and belonging	Interviews	Mathematics students	12	5 F 7 M	UK			10: 19–20 years 2: Mature	1st year UG
Thomas & Quinn	2007	Working class and first generation entry SE who withdraw or at risk of	Participatory: research jury days In-depth interviews		67 interviews		UK		Working class	Under 25	UG

(Continued)

Researchers	Year	Focus	Method[1]	Subjects	Number	Gender[2]	Location[3]	Race/Ethnicity/Nationality	Class	Age	Level
Barrow	2006	SE of assessment	Interviews	Accountancy Design			New Zealand				Final yr UG
Burke & Dunn	2006	SE of reflexive pedagogy	Student journals	Science and engineering	200		UK				Pre-degree
Clegg et al.	2006	SE experience of coping with challenges	Interviews		14	M & F	UK	Ethnically mixed		Mature Younger FT & PT	
Dibben	2006	Socio-cultural and learning experiences	(Surveys) Interviews	Music	41 (survey) 10 interviews	M & F	UK			17–25 yrs	UG
Harrison	2006	SE of negative experiences leading to withdrawal	Telephone survey		151		UK				UG
Hutchings	2006	SE of academic literacy development	Writing centre consultant reports		155	M & F	South Africa	English home language English second language English foreign language			UG & PG
Kimura et al.	2006	Non-traditional SE of HE sector	Institutional case studies Questionnaires Interviews Participant observation	Humanities Social work Nursing Business Computing Sports and education Media Psychosocial	110 interviewed	M & F	UK	Minority ethnic British Asian Pakistani Asian Indian Black White			UG & Graduates

	Year	Focus	Method	Discipline	Sample size	Gender	Country	Ethnicity	Class	Age	Level
Lambert & Parker	2006	SE of anti-sexist activism	Interviews			M & F	UK				UG
Llamas	2006	Student discourses of the 'good student'	Interviews	Law Nursing Psychology Social Work Engineering Education Human Sciences Environmental Sciences English Language	50	M & F	Spain				UG
McClure	2006	SE of black fraternity members on mainly white campus	Interviews	Social Science Humanities Business Science	20	M	USA			19–23 yrs	UG
Moore	2006	SE of changing educational identity	Life history interviews		21	15 F 6 M	Finland				PG Graduates
Moreau & Leathwood	2006	Working class SE of balancing work and study	Longitudinal study (Questionnaires) Interviews Focus groups	Psychology Business Computing Film studies	310 initial sample 18 individual case studies	M & F	UK	White Asian Black	Working class Non-traditional	Under 21 – over 25	UG
Robotham & Julian	2006	Critical review of SE of stress									
Rosado & David	2006	SE of mass higher education	Ethnographic approach Open interviews		40		Spain		Across classes		UG

(Continued)

Researchers	Year	Focus	Method[1]	Subjects	Number	Gender[2]	Location[3]	Race/Ethnicity/Nationality	Class	Age	Level
Severiens et al.	2006	SE of social and academic integration	Interviews	Engineering	138	49 F 89 M	Holland	Dutch Surinam Turkey Morocco			Year 1 Year 4 UGs
White	2006	SE of university	Semi-structured interviews	Arts Professional degrees	79	M & F	Australia	Home students		Under 21	2nd yr UG non-Hons
Case	2005	SE of learning	Interviews and participant observation	Chemical Engineering	36	M & F	South Africa	Black African Coloured Indian White			3rd year UG
Griffiths et al.	2005	SE of 'learning shock'	Questionnaires Interviews	Business Administration	145 24 Ints	M & F	UK	UK students Asia Pacific Europe Rest of the world			PG
O'Neill & Wyness	2005	SE of inter-professional course on HIV/ AIDS	Focus groups Telephone interviews	Social work Nursing Medicine Pharmacology	23	3 M 20 F	Canada				UG
Riddell et al.	2005	Disabled students' experience	Case studies		48	M & F	Scotland England				
Wilcox et al.	2005	SE of first year and choice of staying or leaving	Interviews	Applied social science	34	F 80% M 20%	UK	White 90%		Mature 16%	UG
Zhou	2005	SE of sharing indigenous knowledge in class	Interviews in English or Mandarin		10	5 F 5 M	Canada	Mainland Chinese		25–39	PG

Davis et al.	2004	Black SE at predominantly white university	Phenomenological interviews	Engineering Psychology Accounting Education English	11	7 F 4 M	USA	Black		21–26	Graduating
Guest & Bloomfield	2004	Reasons for going to university + financial circumstances	Journalism – interviews	Arts & Social Science	6	4 F 2 M	UK			Varied	Pre-entry
Tett	2004	Mature working-class SE of elite university	Semi-structured interviews Group interviews	Community education	28	10 M 18 F	Scotland		Working-class	Mature	UG
Lea et al.	2003	SE and attitudes to student-centred learning	Focus groups (+ internet questionnaire)	Psychology	48		UK			Direct entry and mature students	Full time UG & PG
Mann	2003	SE of seminar	Interviews based on selected video clips of one class	Arts	2	F	Scotland			Direct entry	3r & 4th UG
Read et al.	2003	SE of belonging and isolation in HE in post-1992 university	Focus groups from 3 different studies	Science and four discipline areas	175	More than 70% F	UK	White British Asian Black Euro and other	Mostly working class	43% mature	1st yr UG
Gale	2002	SE of students with 'learning disabilities'	(Survey) Semi-structured interviews	Education	115 surveyed 9 interviewed		Australia			Direct entry	1st yr
Glasgow University Guardian	2002	Provocative grafitti to stir up students: 'détournements'	Journalistic interview		1		Scotland				UG

(Continued)

Researchers	Year	Focus	Method[1]	Subjects	Number	Gender[2]	Location[3]	Race/Ethnicity/Nationality	Class	Age	Level
Haggis	2002	SE experience of learning in context of academic writing	Semi-structured interviews	Humanities and social sciences	8	3 M 5 F	UK	White Mixed nationality	Mixed	25–44	Full time PG (taught Masters and PhD)
Harland	2002	SE of collaborative enquiry in PBL	Action-research case study using reflective writing	Zoology	14		Scotland				4th yr
McLelland	2002	Students' embodied experience	Interviews and written accounts		20		USA				UG and PG
Unpublished											
Mann		SE of first year	Weekly study journal	Arts	1	F	Scotland			Mature	1st yr UG
Mann		SE of first year	Semi-structured interview	Arts	1	M	Scotland			Mature	1st yr UG
E. McAteer		SE of Honours choice	Focus group	Arts	12		Scotland				3rd & 4th yr UG

[1] I have indicated in brackets quantitative methods that have also been used as part of a study but which I do not directly draw on in Chapter 3.

[2] Where possible I have included socio-structural information about the subjects of the study, using the terms used by the authors.

[3] I have used UK where it is very likely that the students are studying in England, though this may include Wales, N. Ireland and/or Scotland.

M = male; F = female; PG = postgraduate; UG = undergraduate; FT = full-time; PT = part-time; HE = higher education.

References

Abram, D. (1996) *The Spell of the Sensuous*. New York: Vintage Books.

Ainley, P. (2003) Eight statements of the 'bleeding blindingly obvious' and a PS on education as social control, *British Journal of the Sociology of Education*, 24(3): 347–355.

Allwright, R. (1989) Interaction in the language classroom: social problems and pedagogic possibilities. Paper presented to Les Etats Généraux des Langues, Paris, April 1989.

Althusser, L. (1971) Ideology and ideological state apparatuses, in *Lenin and Philosophy and other Essays*. London: New Left Books.

Anderson, C. (1997) Enabling and shaping understanding through tutorials, in F. Marton, D. Hounsell and N.J. Entwistle (eds) *The Experience of Learning – Implications for Teaching and Studying in Higher Education*, 2nd edn. Edinburgh: Scottish Academic Press.

Anderson, C. and Day, K. (2005) Purposive environments: Engaging students in the values and practices of history, *Higher Education*, 49: 319–343.

Anderson, P. (2001) Betwixt and between: classifying identities in higher education, in P. Anderson and J. Williams (eds) *Identity and Difference in Higher Education*. Aldershot: Ashgate.

Anderson, P. and Williams, J. (2001) Identity and difference: Concepts and themes, in P. Anderson and J. Williams (eds) *Identity and Difference in Higher Education*. Aldershot: Ashgate.

Antonio, A.L. and Muñiz, M. (2007) The sociology of diversity, in P.J. Gumport (ed.) *Sociology of Higher Education – Contributions and Contexts*. Baltimore: John Hopkins University Press.

Apple, M.W. (1979) *Ideology and Curriculum*. London: Routledge and Kegan Paul.

Archer, L. (2004) Re/theorizing 'difference' in feminist research, *Women's Studies International Forum*, 27: 459–473.

Arendt, H. (1993) *Between Past and Future: Eight Exercises in Political Thought*. New York: Penguin.

Arisaka, Y. (2000) Asian women: invisibility, locations and claims to philosophy, in N. Zack (ed.) *Women of Colour and Philosophy: A Critical Reader*. Malden, MA: Blackheath.

Ashenden, S. and Owen, D. (1999) *Foucault contra Habermas*. London: Sage Publications.

Ashwin, P. (2005) Variation in students' experiences of the 'Oxford tutorial', *Higher Education*, 50(4): 631–644.

Ashworth, P., Bannister, P. and Thorne, P. (1998) Four good reasons for cheating and plagiarism, in C. Rust (ed.) *Improving Student Learning Symposium*. Oxford: Oxford Centre for Staff Development, Oxford Brookes University.

Ashworth, P. (2004) Understanding as the transformation of what is already known, *Teaching in Higher Education*, 9(2): 147–158.

Astley, N. (2003) *Staying Alive – Real Poems for Unreal Times*, 5th edn. Northumberland: Bloodaxe Books.

Bakhtin, M. (1981) Discourse in the novel, in M. Holoquist (ed.) *The Dialogic Imagination: Four Essays by M.M. Bakhtin*. Austin: University of Texas Press.

Barnett, R. (1997) *Higher Education: A Critical Business*. Buckingham: SRHE/Open University Press.

Barnett, R. (2005) Recapturing the universal in the university, *Educational Philosophy and Theory*, 37(6): 785–797.

Barr, J. (1999) *Liberating Knowledge – Research, Feminism and Adult Education*. Leicester: NIACE.

Barr, J. and Griffiths, M. (2004) Training the imagination to go visiting, in M. Walker and J. Nixon (eds) *Reclaiming Universities from a Runaway World*. Maidenhead: SRHE/Open University Press.

Barrow, M. (2006) Assessment and student transformation: linking character and intellect, *Studies in Higher Education*, 31(3): 357–372.

Barthes, R. (2000) *Camera Lucida – Reflections on Photography*, translated by R. Howard. London: Vintage.

Bartholomae, D. (1985) Inventing the university, in M. Rose (ed.) *When a Writer Can't Write*. New York: Guildford.

Barton, D. and Tusting, K. (2005) *Beyond Communities of Practice: Language, Power and Social Context*. Cambridge: Cambridge University Press.

Baudrillard, J. (1987) *The Ecstasy of Communication*. New York: Semiotext(e).

Beaty, E., Gibbs, G. and Morgan, A. (1997) Learning orientations and study contracts, in F. Marton, D. Hounsell and N.J. Entwistle (eds) *The Experience of Learning – Implications for Teaching and Studying in Higher Education*, 2nd edn. Edinburgh: Scottish Academic Press.

Becker, H.S. (1995) Making the grade revisited, in H.S. Becker, B. Geer and E.C. Hughes (eds) *Making the Grade: The Academic Side of College Life*, 2nd edn. New Brunswick: Transaction, Inc.

Becker, H.S., Geer, B. and Hughes, E.C. (1968) *Making the Grade: The Academic Side of College Life*. New York: John Wiley and Sons.

Benhabib, S. (1992) *Situating the Self: Gender, Community and Postmodernism in Contemporary Ethics*. Cambridge: Polity Press.

Benjamin, W. (1973) Theses on the philosophy of history, in H. Arendt (ed.) *Illuminations*. London: Fontana.

Bergerson, A.A. (2007) Exploring the impact of social class on adjustment to college: Anna's story, *International Journal of Qualitative Studies in Education*, 20(1): 99–119.

Bernstein, B. (1975) *Class, Codes and Control: Towards a Theory of Education Transmission*, 2nd edn. London: Routledge and Kegan Paul.

Biggs, J. (2003) *Teaching for Quality Learning at University*. Buckingham: SRHE/Open University Press.

Blake, N. and Masschelein, J. (2003) Critical theory and critical pedagogy, in N. Blake,

P. Smeyers, R. Smith and P. Standish (eds) *The Blackwell Guide to the Philosophy of Education.* Oxford: Blackwell Publishing.

Blake, N., Smeyers, P., Smith, R. and Standish, P. (eds) (2003) *The Blackwell Guide to the Philosophy of Education.* Oxford: Blackwell Publishing.

Booth, S. (1997) On phenomenography, learning and teaching, *Higher Education Research and Development,* 16(2): 135–158.

Bourdieu, P. (1988) *Homo Academicus.* Oxford: Polity Press.

Bourdieu, P. (1997) The forms of capital, in A. Halsey, H. Lauder, P. Brown and A. Stuart Wells (eds) *Education: Culture, Economy, and Society.* Oxford: Oxford University Press.

Bourdieu, P. and Passeron, J.-C. (1977) *Reproduction: In Education, Society and Culture,* 2nd edn. London: Sage Publications.

Bourdieu, P., Passeron, J.-C. and De Saint Martin, M. (1994) *Academic Discourse.* Oxford: Polity Press.

Bowl, M. (2003) *Non-traditional Entrants to Higher Education: 'They talk about people like me'.* Stoke on Trent: Trentham Books.

Bowles, S. and Gintis, H. (1976) *Schooling in Capitalist America.* London: Routledge and Kegan Paul.

Breen, M.P. (2001) Navigating the discourse: on what is learned in the language classroom, in C.N. Candlin and N. Mercer (eds) *English Language Teaching in Its Social Context – A Reader.* London: Routledge.

Brew, A. (2006) *Research and Teaching: Beyond the Divide (Universities into the 21st Century).* London: Palgrave Macmillan.

Broadfoot, P. (2000) Preface, in A. Filer (ed.) *Assessment Social Practice and Social Product.* London: Falmer Press.

Burke, P.J. and Dunn, S. (2006) Communicating science: exploring reflexive pedagogical approaches, *Teaching in Higher Education,* 11(2): 219–231.

Callender, C. and Wilkinson, D. (2003) *2002/03 student income and expenditure survey: students' income, expenditure and debt in 2002/03 and changes since 1998/99.* London: Department for Education and Employment.

Callon, M. and Latour, B. (1981) Unscrewing the big leviathan: how actors macrostructure reality and sociologists help them to do so, in K. D. Knorr-Cetina and A. Cicourel (eds) *Advances in Social Theory and Methodology: Towards an Integration of Micro- and Macro-Sociologies.* London: Routledge and Kegan Paul.

Campus Celebrity Enigma (2002) The Graffiti Artist, *Glasgow University Guardian,* 13 November 2002.

Carter, D.F. (2006) Key issues in the persistence of underrepresented minority students, *New Directions for Institutional Research,* 130: 33–46.

Case, J. (2007) Alienation and engagement: exploring students' experiences of studying engineering, *Teaching in Higher Education,* 12(1): 119–133.

Case, J.M. (2005) Alienation and engagement: Empirical evaluation of a new theoretical framework for understanding student learning. Paper presented to Staff and Educational Development Association (SEDA) Spring Conference, Belfast.

Case, J.M. and Gunstone, R.F. (2003) Going deeper than deep and surface approaches: a study of students' perceptions of time, *Teaching in Higher Education,* 8(1): 55–69.

Chouliaraki, L. and Fairclough, N. (1999) *Discourse in Late Modernity – Rethinking Critical Discourse Analysis.* Edinburgh: Edinburgh University Press.

Clegg, S.R. (1989) *Frameworks of Power.* London: Sage Publications.

Clegg, S., Bradley, S. and Smith, K. (2006) 'I've had to swallow my pride': help seeking and self-esteem, *Higher Education Research and Development*, 25(2): 101–113.

Connell, R.W. (1987) *Gender and Power*. Cambridge: Polity Press.

Couldry, N. (2000) *Inside Culture – Re-imagining the Method of Cultural Studies*. London: Sage Publications.

Cousin, G. (2003) Threshold concepts, troublesome knowledge and learning about others. Paper presented to the 10th Conference of the European Association for Research on Learning and Instruction (EARLI), Padova, Italy, 26–30 August 2003.

Cousin, G. (2006) Beyond saris, samosas and steel bands, *Exchange*, 5(winter): 34–35.

Cranmer, S. (2006) Enhancing graduate employability: best intentions and mixed outcomes, *Studies in Higher Education*, 31(2): 169–184.

Davis, M. and Wallbridge, D. (1983) *Boundary and Space – An Introduction to the Work of D.W. Winnicott*. Harmondsworth: Penguin Education.

Davis, M., Dias-Bowie, Y., Greenberg, K., Klukken, G., Pollio, H.R., Thomas, S.P. and Thompson, C.L. (2004) 'A fly in the buttermilk': Descriptions of university life by successful black undergraduate students at a predominantly white southeastern university, *Journal of Higher Education*, 75(4): 420–445.

Delanty, G. (2001) *Challenging Knowledge – The University in the Knowledge Society*. Buckingham: SRHE and Open University Press.

Deleuze, G. and Guattari, F. (1987) *A Thousand Plateaus: Capitalism and Schizophrenia*. Minneapolis: University of Minnesota Press.

Dibben, N. (2006) The socio-cultural and learning experiences of music students in a British university, *British Journal of Music Education*, 23(1): 91–116.

Duke, C. (2004) Is there an Australian idea of a university? *Journal of Higher Education Policy and Management*, 26(3): 297–314.

Eagleton, T. (1994) The intellectual as hero, *The Guardian Weekly*, 1 May 1994.

Elton, L.R.B. and Laurillard, D. (1979) Trends in research on student learning, *Studies in Higher Education*, 4(1): 87–102.

Entwistle, N.J. (1997) Contrasting perspectives on learning, in F. Marton, D. Hounsell and N.J. Entwistle (eds) *The Experience of Learning – Implications for Teaching and Studying in Higher Education*, 2nd edn. Edinburgh: Scottish Academic Press.

Entwistle, N.J. (2005) Enhancing teaching-learning environments in undergraduate courses in electronic engineering: an introduction to the ETL project, *International Journal of Electrical Engineering Education*, 42(1): 1–7.

Entwistle, N.J. and McCune, V. (2004) The conceptual bases of study strategy inventories, *Educational Psychology Review*, 16(4): 325–345.

Entwistle, N.J. and Ramsden, P. (1983) *Understanding Student Learning*. London: Croom Helm.

Entwistle, N.J., Hanley, M. and Hounsell, D. (1979) Identifying distinctive approaches to studying, *Higher Education*, 8: 365–380.

Erlich, V. (2004) The 'new' students. The studies and social life of French university students in a context of mass higher education, *European Journal of Education*, 39(4): 485–495.

Evans, M. (2004) *Killing Thinking – Death of the University*. London: Continuum Education.

Fairclough, N.L. (1989) *Language and Power*. London: Longman.

Fairclough, N.L. (1992) *Discourse and Social Change*. Cambridge: Polity Press.

Fairclough, N.L. (1995) *Critical Discourse Analysis*. London: Longman.

Fairclough, N.L. (2003) *Analysing Discourse: Textual Analysis for Social Research*. London: Routledge.

Flower, L. and Hayes, J. (1981) A cognitive process theory of writing, *College Composition and Communication*, 32: 365–387.

Forsyth, A. and Furlong, A. (2003) *Losing Out? Socioeconomic Disadvantage and Experience in Further and Higher Education*. Bristol: Policy Press.

Foucault, M. (1972) *The Archaeology of Knowledge*. London: Tavistock.

Foucault, M. (1979) *Discipline and Punish – The Birth of the Prison*. Harmondsworth: Penguin.

Foucault, M. (1980) Truth and power, in C. Gordon (ed.) *Power/Knowledge: Selected Interviews and Other Writings 1972–1977*. New York: Pantheon Books.

Foucault, M. (1981) Questions of method: an interview with Michel Foucault, *Ideology and Consciousness*, 8: 1–14.

Foucault, M. (1988) *The History of Sexuality, Vol II, The Use of Pleasure*. Harmondsworth: Penguin.

Foucault, M. (1991) Space, knowledge and power, in P. Rabinow (ed.) *The Foucault Reader – An Introduction to Foucault's Thought*. London: Penguin Books, pp. 239–256.

Foucault, M. (1999) Space, power and knowledge, in S. During (ed.) *The Cultural Studies Reader*, 2nd edn. London: Routledge.

Fowler, R., Hodge, B., Kress, G. and Trew, T. (1979) *Language and Control*. London: Routledge and Kegan Paul.

Fransson, A. (1977) On qualitative differences in learning IV – Effects of motivation and test anxiety on process and outcome, *British Journal of Educational Psychology*, 47: 244–257.

Freire, P. (1970) Cultural action for freedom, *Harvard Educational Review*, Monograph Series No. 1.

Freire, P. (1973) *Education for Critical Consciousness*. New York: Seabury.

Freire, P. (1996) *Pedagogy of the Oppressed*, twentieth anniversary edn. London: Penguin Books.

Frow, J. (1995) *Cultural Studies and Cultural Value*. Oxford: Clarendon Press.

Gale, T. (2002) Degrees of difficulty: an ecological account of learning in Australian higher education, *Studies in Higher Education*, 27(1): 66–78.

Garrison, J. and Neiman, A. (2003) Pragmatism and education, in N. Blake, P. Smeyers, R. Smith and P. Standish (eds) *The Blackwell Guide to the Philosophy of Education*. Oxford: Blackwell Publishing.

Gee, J.P. (1990) *Social Linguistics and Literacies: Ideology in Discourse*. London: Falmer Press.

Giddens, A. (1991) *Modernity and Self-Identity*. Cambridge: Polity Press.

Gill, S. (2007) Overseas students' intercultural adaptation as intercultural learning: a transformative framework, *Compare*, 37(2): 167–183.

Giroux, H. (1983) *Theory and Resistance in Education – A Pedagogy for the Opposition*. London: Heinemann Educational Books.

Goffman, E. (1961) *Asylums*. Harmondsworth: Penguin.

Goode, J. (2007) 'Managing' disability: early experiences of university students with disabilities, *Disability and Society*, 22(1): 35–48.

Gore, J. (1993) *The Struggle for Pedagogies: Critical and Feminist Discourses as Regimes of Truth*. London: Routledge.

Gough, B. and Madill, A. (2007) *Diversity and Subjectivity within Qualitative Sociology*, NCRM Working Paper Series 1/07, University of Leeds: ESRC National Centre for Research Methods.

Gramsci, A. (1971) *Selections from Prison Notebooks*. London: Lawrence and Wishart.

Greasley, K. and Ashworth, P. (2007) The phenomenology of 'approach to studying': the university student's studies within the lifeworld, *British Educational Research Journal,* 33(6): 819–843.

Griffiths, D.S., Winstanley, D. and Gabriel, Y. (2005) Learning shock: the trauma of return to formal learning, *Management Learning,* 36(3): 275–297.

Guest, K. and Bloomfield, S. (2004) Generation U: who are they, what do they want (and can they afford it)? *Independent on Sunday,* 26 September 2004.

Habermas, J.G. (1971) Technology and science in ideology, in *Toward a Rational Society: Student Protest, Science, and Politics,* translated by Jeremy J. Shapiro. London: Heinemann.

Habermas, J.G. (1973) *Legitimation and Crisis.* Boston: Beacon Press.

Habermas, J.G. (1984) *The Theory of Communicative Action, Vol 1: Reason and the Rationalization of Society.* Boston: Beacon Press.

Habermas, J.G. (1987) *The Theory of Communicative Action, Vol. 2: Lifeworld and System: A Critique of Functionalist Reason.* Boston: Beacon Press.

Habermas, J.G. (1989) *The New Conservatism.* Cambridge, MA: MIT Press.

Haggis, T. (2002) Exploring the 'black box' of process: a comparison of theoretical notions of the 'adult learner' with accounts of postgraduate learning experience, *Studies in Higher Education,* 27(2): 207–220.

Haggis, T. (2006) Pedagogies for diversity: retaining critical challenge amidst fears of 'dumbing down', *Studies in Higher Education,* 31(5): 521–535.

Hall, S. (1988) The toad in the garden: Thatcherism among the theorists, in C. Nelson and L. Grossberg (eds) *Marxism and the Interpretation of Culture.* Basingstoke: Macmillan.

Hall, S. (1992) Our mongrel selves, *New Statesman and Society,* 19 June 1992.

Halliwell, M. and Mousley, A. (2003) *Critical Humanisms: Humanist/Anti-Humanist Dialogues.* Edinburgh: Edinburgh University Press.

Hand, S. (1989) *The Levinas Reader.* Oxford: Blackwell Publishing.

Hannerz, U. (1992) *Cultural Complexity: Studies in the Social Organization of Meaning.* New York: Columbia University Press.

Harland, T. (2002) Zoology students' experiences of collaborative enquiry in problem-based learning, *Teaching in Higher Education,* 7(1): 3–15.

Harrison, N. (2006) The impact of negative experiences, dissatisfaction and attachment on first year undergraduate withdrawal, *Journal of Further and Higher Education,* 30(4): 377–391.

Harvey, L., Drew, S. and Smith, M. (2006) The first-year experience, in M. Prosser (ed.) *Academy Literature Reviews 2005/06 Executive Summaries.* York: Higher Education Academy.

Hebel, S. (2007) The graduation gap, *Chronicle of Higher Education,* 53(29): A20–A21.

Heikkilä, A. and Lonka, K. (2006) Studying in higher education: students' approaches to learning, self-regulation, and cognitive strategies, *Studies in Higher Education,* 31(1): 99–117.

HESA (2007) Press Release 111, http://www.hesa.ac.uk/index.php/content/view/291/161/ (accessed 23 May 2008).

HESA (2008) Press Release 118, http://www.hesa.ac.uk/index.php/content/view/1120/161/ (accessed 23 May 2008).

Hirst, P. (1996) The demands of professional practice and preparation for teaching, in J. Furlong and R. Smith (eds.) *The Role of Higher Education in Initial Teacher Education.* London: Kogan Page, pp. 166–178.

Hirst, P. and Peters, R. (1970) *The Logic of Education.* London: Routledge and Kegan Paul.

Hodgson, V.E. (1997) Lectures and the experience of relevance, in F. Marton, D. Hounsell and N.J. Entwistle (eds) *The Experience of Learning – Implications for Teaching and Studying in Higher Education,* 2nd edn. Edinburgh: Scottish Academic Press.

Hofer, B.K. (2001) Personal epistemology research: Implications for learning and teaching, *Journal of Educational Psychology Review,* 13(4): 353–383.

Hoffman, E. (1989) *Lost in Translation.* London: Vintage.

Holt, J. (1964) *How Children Fail.* Harmondsworth: Penguin Books.

Horowitz, H.L. (1987) *Campus Life: Undergraduate Cultures from the End of the Eighteenth Century to the Present.* New York: Alfred A. Knopf.

Hounsell, D. (1997) Contrasting conceptions of essay-writing, in F. Marton, D. Hounsell and N.J. Entwistle (eds) *The Experience of Learning – Implications for Teaching and Studying in Higher Education,* 2nd edn. Edinburgh: Scottish Academic Press.

Houston, M. and Lebeau, Y. (2006) *The social mediation of university learning,* Working Paper 3, The SOMUL Project, TLRP/ESRC, www.open.ac.uk/cheri/somul-home.htm (accessed 19 November 2007).

Hsieh, M.-H. (2007) Challenges for international students in higher education: one student's narrated story of invisibility and struggle, *College Student Journal,* 41(2): 379–391.

Hutchings, C. (2006) Reaching students: lessons from a writing centre, *Higher Education Research and Development,* 25(3): 247–261.

Hutton, W. (1995) *The State We are In: Why Britain is in Crisis and How to Overcome It.* London: Jonathan Cape.

Illich, I. (1976) *Deschooling Society.* Harmondsworth: Pelican Books.

Ivanič, R. (1998) *Writing and Identity: The Discoursal Construction of Identity in Academic Writing.* Amsterdam: Benjamins.

Ivanič, R. (2006) Language, learning and identity, in R. Kiely, P. Rea-Dickins, H. Woodfield and G. Clibbon (eds) *Language, Culture and Identity in Applied Linguistics.* London: British Association for Applied Linguistics/Equinox.

Jackson, P. (1968) *Life in Classrooms.* New York: Holt, Rinehart & Winston.

James, C. (1968) *Young Lives at Stake.* Glasgow: Collins.

Jamie, K. (2002) The way we live, in *Mr and Mrs Scotland are Dead: Poems 1980–1994.* Northumberland: Bloodaxe Books.

Jenkins, R. (1996) *Social Identity.* London: Routledge.

Johnson, A.C. (2007) Unintended consequences: how science professors discourage women of color, *Science Education,* 91(5): 805–821.

Kearney, R. and Rainwater, M. (1996) *The Continental Philosophy Reader.* London: Routledge.

Kimura, M., Brain, K., Ganga, D., Hudson, T., Murray, L., Prodgers, L., Smith, K., Straker, K. and Willott, J. (2006) *Ethnicity, Education and Employment.* University of East London: Continuum – The Centre for Widening Participation Policy Studies.

Kitto, S. and Saltmarsh, S. (2007) The production of 'proper cheating' in online examinations within technological universities, *International Journal of Qualitative Studies in Education,* 20(2): 151–171.

Kreber, C. (2006) Setting the context: the climate of university teaching and learning, *New Directions for Higher Education,* 13: 5–11.

Kristeva, J. (1986) Women's time, in T. Moi (ed.) *The Kristeva Reader.* Oxford: Blackwell Publishing.

Lacey, C. (1970) *Hightown Grammar: the School as a Social System.* Manchester: Manchester University Press.

Lambert, C. and Parker, A. (2006) Imagination, hope and the positive face of feminism: pro/feminist pedagogy in 'post' feminist times? *Studies in Higher Education,* 31(4): 469–482.

Lash, S. (1998) Being after time: towards a politics of melancholy, in S. Lash, A. Quick and R. Roberts (eds) *Time and Value.* Oxford: Blackwell Publishing.

Lash, S., Quick, A. and Roberts, R. (1998) *Time and Value.* Oxford: Blackwell Publishing.

Laurillard, D. (1978) A study of the relationship between some of the cognitive and contextual factors in student learning. PhD thesis, University of Surrey.

Lave, J. and Wenger, E. (1991) *Situated Learning, Legitimate Peripheral Participation.* Cambridge: Cambridge University Press.

Lea, M. and Street, B. (1998) Student writing in higher education: An academic literacies approach, *Studies in Higher Education,* 23(2): 157–172.

Lea, M.L. (2005) 'Communities of practice' in higher education: useful heuristic or educational model? in D. Barton and K. Tusting (eds) *Beyond Communities of Practice – Language, Power, and Social Context.* Cambridge: Cambridge University Press.

Lea, S.J., Stephenson, D. and Troy, J. (2003) Higher education students' attitudes to student-centred learning: beyond 'educational bulimia'? *Studies in Higher Education,* 28(3): 321–334.

Leathwood, C. and O'Connell, P. (2003) 'It's a struggle': the construction of the 'new student' in higher education, *Journal of Educational Policy,* 18(6): 597–615.

Lechte, J. (1994) *Fifty Key Contemporary Thinkers: from Structuralism to Postmodernity.* London: Routledge.

Lee, J.J. and Rice, C. (2007) Welcome to America? International student perceptions of discrimination, *Higher Education,* 53(3): 381–409.

Letherby, G. and Shiels, J. (2001) 'Isn't he good, but can we take her seriously?': gendered expectations in higher education, in P. Anderson and J. Williams (eds) *Identity and Difference in Higher Education.* Aldershot: Ashgate.

Lezard, N. (2004) Review of Albion: the Origins of the English Imagination, *The Guardian Review,* 31 July 2004.

Lillis, T.M. (2001) *Student Writing: Access, Regulation and Desire.* London: Routledge.

Lingis, A. (1998) Catastrophic times, in S. Lash, A. Quick and R. Roberts (eds) *Time and Value.* Oxford: Blackwell Publishing.

Llamas, J.M.C. (2006) Technologies of disciplinary power in action: the norm of the 'good student', *Higher Education,* 52: 665–686.

Longden, B. (2006) An institutional response to changing student expectations and their impact on retention rates, *Journal of Higher Education Policy and Management,* 28(2): 173–187.

Lukes, S. (1967) Alienation and anomie, in P. Laslett and W.G. Runciman (eds) *Philosophy, Politics and Society.* Oxford: Basil Blackwell.

Lukes, S. (1974) *Power: A Radical View.* London: Macmillan.

Maassen, P. and Cloete, N. (2006) Global reform trends in higher education, in N. Cloete, P. Maassen, R. Fehnel, T. Moja, T. Gibbon and H. Perold (eds) *Transformation in Higher Education – Global Pressures and Local Realities.* Dordrecht: Springer.

Maclachlan, K. (2007) Learning for democracy in undemocratic places: reflections from within higher education, *Concept*, 17(3): 8–12.

Mann, S.J. (2000) The student's experience of reading, *Higher Education*, 39(3): 297–317.

Mann, S.J. (2001) Alternative perspectives on the student experience: alienation and engagement, *Studies in Higher Education*, 26(1): 7–19.

Mann, S.J. (2003) Inquiring into a higher education classroom: insights into the different perspectives of teacher and students, in C. Rust (ed.) *Improving Student Learning Theory and Practice – 10 Years On*. Oxford: Oxford Brookes University.

Mann, S.J. (2005) Alienation in the learning environment: a failure of community? *Studies in Higher Education*, 30(1): 43–55.

Margolis, E. (ed.) (2001) *Hidden Curriculum in Higher Education*. London: RoutledgeFalmer.

Margolis, E., Soldatenko, M., Acker, S. and Gair, M. (2001) Peekaboo, in E. Margolis (ed.) *The Hidden Curriculum in Higher Education*. London: Routledge Falmer.

Marshall, D. and Case, J. (2005) 'Approaches to learning' research in higher education: a response to Haggis, *British Educational Research Journal*, 31(2): 257–267.

Marton, F. (1981) Phenomenography – describing conceptions of the world around us, *Instructional Science*, 10: 177–200.

Marton, F., Hounsell, D. and Entwistle, N. J. (eds) (1997) *The Experience of Learning Implications for Teaching and Studying in Higher Education*, 2nd edn. Edinburgh: Scottish Academic Press.

Marton, F. and Saljo, R. (1976) On qualitative differences in learning: I – Outcome and process, *British Journal of Educational Psychology*, 46: 4–11.

Marton, F. and Saljo, R. (1997) Approaches to learning, in F. Marton, D. Hounsell and N.J. Entwistle (eds) *The Experience of Learning – Implications for Teaching and Studying in Higher Education*, 2nd edn. Edinburgh: Scottish Academic Press.

Marx, K. (1976) *Capital: A Critique of Political Economy*. London: Penguin.

Mayne, M. (2001) *Learning to Dance*. London: Darton, Longman & Todd.

Mayuzumi, K., Motobayashi, K., Nagayama, C. and Takeuchi, M. (2007) Transforming diversity in Canadian higher education: a dialogue of Japanese women graduate students, *Teaching in Higher Education*, 12(5/6): 581–592.

McClelland, J., Dahlberg, K. and Plihal, J. (2002) Learning in the Ivory Tower: students' embodied experience, *College Teaching*, 50(1): 4–8.

McClure, S.M. (2006) Voluntary association membership: Black Greek men on a predominantly white campus, *Journal of Higher Education*, 77(6): 1036–1057.

McCune, V. and Hounsell, D. (2005) The development of students' ways of thinking and practising in three final-year biology courses, *Higher Education*, 49: 255–289.

McDonough, P.M. and Fann, A.J. (2007) The study of inequality, in P.J. Gumport (ed.) *Sociology of Higher Education – Contributions and their Contexts*. Baltimore: John Hopkins University Press.

McLaren, P. (1980) *Cries from the Corridor*. London: Methuen.

McLaren, P. (2003) *Life in Schools – An Introduction to Critical Pedagogy in the Foundations of Education*, 4th edn. Boston: Allyn and Bacon.

McLean, M. (2006) *Pedagogy and the University – Critical Theory and Practice*. London: Continuum.

Meighan, R. and Siraj-Blatchford, I. (2003) *A Sociology of Educating*, 4th edn. London: Continuum.

Meyer, J.H.F. and Land, R. (2003) Threshold concepts and troublesome knowledge (1): Linkages to ways of thinking and practising, in C. Rust (ed.) *Improving*

Student Learning. Improving Student Learning Theory and Practice Ten Years On. Oxford: OCSLD.

Meyer, J.H.F. and Land, R. (2005) Threshold concepts and troublesome knowledge (2): Epistemological considerations and a conceptual framework for teaching and learning, *Higher Education*, 49: 373–388.

Miclea, M. (2004) 'Learning to Do' as a pillar of education and its links to entrepreneurial studies in higher education: European contexts and approaches, *Higher Education in Europe*, XXIX(2): 221–231.

Miller, C.M.L. and Parlett, M. (1974) *Up to the Mark: a study of the examination game.* London: SRHE.

Moore, E. (2006) Educational identities of adult university graduates, *Scandinavian Journal of Educational Research*, 50(2): 149–163.

Moreau, M.-P. and Leathwood, C. (2006a) Balancing paid work and studies: working (-class) students in higher education, *Studies in Higher Education*, 31(1): 23–42.

Moreau, M.-P and Leathwood, C. (2006b) Graduates' employment and the discourse of employability: a critical analysis, *Journal of Education and Work*, 19(4): 305–324.

Morgan, A. and Beaty, E. (1997) The world of the learner, in F. Marton, D. Hounsell and N. J. Entwistle (eds) *The Experience of Learning – Implications for Teaching and Studying in Higher Education*, 2nd edn. Edinburgh: Scottish Academic Press.

Morrow, R.A. and Torres, C.A. (2002) *Reading Freire and Habermas. Critical Pedagogy and Transformative Social Change.* New York: Teachers College Press.

Moss, D. (2004) Creating space for learning: conceptualizing women and higher education through space and time, *Gender and Education*, 16(3): 283–302.

Norton, L.S., Richardson, J.T.E., Hartley, J., Newstead, S. and Mayes, J. (2005) Teachers' beliefs and intentions concerning teaching in higher education, *Higher Education*, 50/4: 537–571.

O'Leary, T. (2002) *Foucault and the Art of Ethics.* London: Continuum Books.

Olsen, T. (1985) *Silences*, 3rd edn. London: Virago.

O'Neill, B.J. and Wyness, M.A. (2005) Student voices on an interprofessional course, *Medical Teacher*, 27(5): 433–438.

Outhwaite, W. (1996) *The Habermas Reader.* Oxford: Polity Press.

Parlett, M. (1977) The department as a learning milieu, *Studies in Higher Education*, 2(2): 173–181.

Peseta, T. (2007) Revisiting curriculum again: learning and becoming as a new academic developer, *HERDSA Conference 2007*.

Porter, S.R. and Swing, R.L. (2006) Understanding how first-year seminars affect persistence, *Research in Higher Education*, 47(1): 89–109.

Powers, R. (2004) Real time bandits, *The Guardian Saturday Review*, 14 August 2004.

Probyn, E. (1993) *Sexing the Self.* London: Routledge.

Prosser, M. (2005) Interpreting the results of student evaluation, *Higher Education Academy*, http://www.heacademy.ac.uk/5530.htm (accessed 15 May 2007).

Prosser, M. and Trigwell, K. (1999) *Understanding Learning and Teaching: The Experience in Higher Education.* Buckingham: SRHE and Open University Press.

Rabinow, P. (1991) *The Foucault Reader.* Harmondsworth: Penguin Books.

Ramsden, P. (1992) *Learning to Teach in Higher Education.* London: Kogan Page.

Ramsden, P. (1997) The context of learning in academic departments, in F. Marton, D. Hounsell and N. Entwistle (eds) *The Experience of Learning. Implications for Teaching and Studying in Higher Education*, 2nd edn. Edinburgh: Scottish Academic Press.

Rassmussen, D.M. (1990) *Reading Habermas*. Oxford: Basil Blackwell.

Read, B., Francis, B. and Robson, J. (2001) 'Playing safe': Undergraduate essay writing and the presentation of the student 'voice', *British Journal of Sociology of Education*, 22(3): 387–399.

Read, B., Archer, L. and Leathwood, C. (2003) Challenging cultures? Student conceptions of 'belonging' and 'isolation' at a post-1992 university, *Studies in Higher Education*, 28(3): 261–277.

Riddell, S., Tinklin, T. and Wilson, A. (2005) New Labour, social justice and disabled students in higher education, *British Educational Research Journal*, 31(5): 623–643.

Robotham, D. and Julian, C. (2006) Stress and the higher education student: a critical review of the literature, *Journal of Further and Higher Education*, 30(2): 107–177.

Rogers, C.R. and Freiberg, H.J. (1994) *Freedom to Learn*, 3rd edition. New Jersey: Prentice Hall.

Rosado, D.L. and David, M. (2006) 'A massive university or a university for the masses?' Continuity and change in higher education in Spain and in England, *Journal of Educational Policy*, 21(3): 343–365.

Säfström, C.A. (2003) Teaching otherwise, *Studies in Philosophy and Education*, 22(1): 19–30.

Saljo, R. (1979) *Learning in the Learner's Perspective. I. Some Common-sense Conceptions*, 76, Göteborg: University of Göteborg.

Saljo, R. (1997) Reading and everyday conceptions of knowledge, in F. Marton, D. Hounsell and N. Entwistle (eds) *The Experience of Learning – Implications for Teaching and Studying in Higher Education*, 2nd edn. Edinburgh: Scottish Academic Press.

Sartre, J.-P. (1956) *Being and Nothingness*. New York: Philosophical Library.

Sarup, M. (1978) *Marxism and Education: A Study of Phenomenological and Marxist Approaches to Education*. London: Routledge and Kegan Paul.

Sarup, M. (1996) *Identity, Culture and the Postmodern World*. Edinburgh: Edinburgh University Press.

Schact, R. (1971) *Alienation*. London: George Allen and Unwin.

Schuller, T. (1999) Contribution to Adult Education for Democratic Renewal in Scotland, Fourth Edinburgh Biennial Adult Education Conference, University of Edinburgh, 13 March 1999.

Scott, J.C. (1985) *Weapons of the Weak: Everyday Forms of Peasant Resistance*. New Haven: Yale University Press.

Seeman, M. (1983) Alienation motifs in contemporary theorizing: the hidden continuity of the classic themes, *Social Psychology Quarterly*, 46: 171–184.

Severiens, S., ten Dam, G. and Blom, S. (2006) Comparison of Dutch ethnic minority and majority engineering students: social and academic integration, *International Journal of Inclusive Education*, 10(1): 75–89.

Sissel, P.A., Hansman, C.A. and Kasworm, C.E. (2001) The politics of neglect: adult learners in higher education, *New Directions for Adult and Continuing Education*, 91(fall).

Smail, D. (1987) *Taking Care: An Alternative to Therapy*. London: J.M. Dent and Sons.

Snyder, B.R. (1966) The hidden curriculum, in L. Pervin (ed.) *The College Dropout*. Princeton: Princeton University Press.

Solomon, Y. (2007) Not belonging? What makes a functional learner identity in undergraduate mathematics, *Studies in Higher Education*, 32(1): 79–96.

Spivak, G. (1990) *The Postcolonial Critic: Interviews, Strategies, Dialogues*. New York: Routledge.

Surridge, P. (2007a) *The National Student Survey 2006: Summary Report to Higher Education Funding Council for England*, University of Bristol, UK.

Surridge, P. (2007b) *The National Student Survey 2006: Report to Higher Education Funding Council for England*, University of Bristol, UK.

Svensson, L. (1997) Skill in learning and organising knowledge, in F. Marton, D. Hounsell and N. Entwistle (eds) *The Experience of Learning. Implications for Teaching and Studying in Higher Education*, 2nd edn. Edinburgh: Scottish Academic Press.

Swaner, L.E. (2007) Linking engaged learning, student mental health and well-being, and civic development, *Liberal Education*, Winter 2007, 16–25.

Swann, J. (2003) A Popperian approach to research on learning and method, in J. Swann and J. Pratt (eds) *Educational Research in Practice Making Sense of Methodology*. London: Continuum.

Taking Liberties Collective (1989) *Learning the Hard Way. Women's Oppression in Men's Education*. London: Macmillan.

Taylor, C. (1991) *The Ethics of Authenticity*. Cambridge, MA: Harvard University Press.

Taylor, R., Barr, J. and Steele, T. (2002) *For a Radical Higher Education After Postmodernism*. Buckingham: SRHE/Open University Press.

Terkel, S. (2003) *Hope Dies Last – Making a Difference in an Indifferent World*. London: Granta Books.

Tett, L. (2004) Mature working-class students in an 'elite' university: Discourses of risk, choice and exclusion, *Studies in the Education of Adults*, 36(2): 252–264.

Thomas, L. and Quinn, J. (2007) *First Generation Entry into Higher Education – An International Study*. Maidenhead: SRHE and Open University Press.

Thompson, J.B. (1981) *Critical Hermeneutics: A Study in the Thought of Paul Ricoeur and Jurgen Habermas*. Cambridge: Cambridge University Press.

Tlili, A. and Wright, S. (2005) Learn to consume, teach to account? *Anthropology in Action*, 12(1): 64–77.

Tocqueville, A. de (1981) *De la Démocratie en Amérique*. Paris: Garnier-Flammarion.

UNESCO (2006) *Global Education Digest 2006: Comparing Education Statistics Across the World*. Montreal: UNESCO Institute for Statistics.

Vermunt, J.D. (2005) Relations between student learning patterns and personal and contextual factors and academic performance, *Higher Education*, 49: 205–234.

Wacquant, L. (1998) Pierre Bourdieu, in R. Stones (ed.) *Key Sociological Thinkers*. New York: New York University Press.

Walker, M. (2006) *Higher Education Pedagogies*. Maidenhead: SRHE/Open University Press.

Washburn, J. (2005) *University, Inc: The Corporate Corruption of Higher Education*. New York: Basic Books.

Webb, S. (2001) 'I'm Doing It for All of Us': gender and identity in the transition to higher education, in P. Anderson and J. Williams (eds) *Identity and Difference in Higher Education*. Aldershot: Ashgate.

Weil, S.W. (1993) Access: towards education or miseducation? – Adults imagine the future, in M. Thorpe, R. Edwards and A. Hanson (eds) *Culture and Processes of Adult Learning*. London: Routledge with Open University.

Wenger, E. (1998) *Communities of Practice: Learning, Meaning and Identity*. Cambridge: Cambridge University Press.

West, L. (1996) *Adults' Motivation and Higher Education: Beyond Fragments*. London: Taylor & Francis.

White, N.R. (2006) Tertiary education in the noughties: the student perspective, *Higher Education Research and Development*, 25(3): 231–246.

Wilcox, P., Winn, S. and Fyvie-Gauld, M. (2005) 'It was nothing to do with the university, it was just the people': the role of social support in the first-year experience of higher education, *Studies in Higher Education*, 30(6): 707–722.

Williams, R. (1961) *The Long Revolution*. Harmondsworth: Penguin.

Williams, R. (1989) The future of cultural studies, in *The Politics of Modernism: Against the New Conformists*. London: Verso.

Willis, P. (1977) *Learning to Labour: How Working Class Kids Get Working Class Jobs*. Farnborough: Saxon House.

Winnicott, D.W. (1971) *Playing and Reality*. London: Tavistock.

Woods, P. (1990) *The Happiest Days? How Pupils Cope with School*. Basingstoke: Falmer Press.

Yorke, M. and Longden, B. (2007) *The First-year Experience in Higher Education in the UK – Report on Phase 1*. York: Higher Education Academy.

Young, M.F.D. (1971) *Knowledge and Control*. London: Collier-Macmillan.

Zhou, Y.R., Knokke, D. and Sakamoto, I. (2005) Rethinking silence in the classroom: Chinese students' experience of sharing indigenous knowledge, *International Journal of Inclusive Education*, 9(3): 287–311.

INDEX

[Page numbers in italics refer to a figure or table.]

Related books from Open University Press

Purchase from www.openup.co.uk or order through your local bookseller

---

LEARNING SPACES
CREATING OPPORTUNITIES FOR KNOWLEDGE
CREATION IN ACADEMIC LIFE

Maggi Savin-Baden

This is a timely and important book which seeks to reclaim universities as places of learning. It is jargon free and forcefully argued. It should be on every principal and vice-chancellor's list of essential reading.

Jon Nixon, Professor of Educational Studies, University of Sheffield

The ability to have or to find space in academic life seems to be increasingly difficult since we seem to be consumed by teaching and bidding, overwhelmed by emails and underwhelmed by long arduous meetings. This book explores the concept of learning spaces, the idea that there are diverse forms of spaces within the life and life world of the academic where opportunities to reflect and critique their own unique learning position occur.

Learning Spaces sets out to challenge the notion that academic thinking can take place in cramped, busy working spaces, and argues instead for a need to recognise and promote new opportunities for learning spaces to emerge in academic life. The book examines the ideas that:

- Learning spaces are increasingly absent in academic life
- The creation and re-creation of learning spaces is vital for the survival of the academic community
- The absence of learning spaces is resulting in increasing dissolution and fragmentation of academic identities
- Learning spaces need to be valued and possibly redefined in order to regain and maintain the intellectual health of academe

In offering possibilities for creative learning spaces, this innovative book provides key reading for those interested in the future of universities including educational developers, researchers, managers and policy makers.

Contents

2007   184pp
978–0–335–22230–8 (Paperback)   978–0–335–22231–5 (Hardback)

A WILL TO LEARN
BEING A STUDENT IN AN AGE OF UNCERTAINTY

Ronald Barnett

There is an extraordinary but largely unnoticed phenomenon in higher education: by and large, students persevere and complete their studies. How should we interpret this tendency? Students are living in uncertain times and often experience anxiety, and yet they continue to press forward with their studies. The argument here is that we should understand this propensity on the part of students to persist through *a will to learn*.

This book examines the structure of what it is to have a will to learn. Here, a language of being, becoming, authenticity, dispositions, voice, air, spirit, inspiration and care is drawn on. As such, this book offers an idea of student development that challenges the dominant views of our age, of curricula understood largely in terms of skill or even of knowledge, and pedagogy understood as bringing off pre-specified 'outcomes'.

The will to learn, though, can be fragile. This is of crucial importance, for if the will to learn dissolves, the student's commitment may falter. Accordingly, more than encouraging an interest in the student's subject or in the acquiring of skills, the *primary* responsibility of teachers in higher education is to sustain and develop the student's will to learn. This is a radical thesis, for it implies a transformation in how we understand the nature of teaching in higher education.

Contents
Acknowledgements – Introduction – Part 1: Being and becoming – Where there's a will – Being – Authenticity – Becoming – Part 2: Being a student – Travel broadens the mind – A will to offer – Voice – Dispositions and qualities – Part 3: Being a teacher – The inspiring teacher – A pedagogy for uncertain times – Space and risk – A critical spirit – Coda: Puzzles and possibilities – Notes – Bibliography – Subject index – Name index.

2007   208pp
978–0–335–22380–0 (Paperback)   978–0–335–22381–7 (Hardback)